To
Gordon McDonald
&
Bill Gaither
who stay my friends
even when they disagree
with my thinking

Contents

Acknowledgments xi
Introduction xiii
Note to International Readers xvii

1. Is Jesus a Republican or a Democrat? *1*

2. Do Real Christians Smoke? *17*

3. Do Christians Promote Gay-Bashing? *25*

4. Are Christian Talk Shows Christian? *39*

5. What Should We Do with Illegal Aliens, or *49*
   Is Proposition 187 Christian?

6. Does God Have a Feminine Side? *55*

7. What about Prayer in Public Schools? *65*

8. Should Christians Quit Teaching in *75*
   the Public School System?

9. Is Television Demonic? *85*

10. Is That Preacher Who Killed the Abortion *97*
    Doctor Guilty of Murder?

11. Was Jesus a Moderate? *105*

12. Should Christians Support Gun Control? *115*

13. Is Christian Environmentalism an Oxymoron? *123*

14. Do Christians Have a Right to *135*
Take Over America?

A Brief Introduction to the Next Two Chapters *147*

15. Does God Prefer Poor People? *149*

16. What Should Christians Do about *159*
the Welfare System?

Conclusion: Should Christians Avoid Controversy? *171*

P.S. *181*

Acknowledgments

WHEN WRITING a book, it is customary to cite all of those who made the author's work possible. First and foremost is my wife, Peggy, whose editing of this manuscript included but was not limited to correcting my bad grammar. Laura Kendall, my editor at Word Publishing, did everything an editor is supposed to do—and did it well.

My friend, Sue Dahlstrom, was responsible for getting the manuscript from the yellow legal pads on which I wrote it onto the computer disks my publisher requires. She did most of the typing and helped with my research, and I am grateful for her willingness to work as hard as I did to meet deadlines.

My secretary, Diana Robertson, did typing and a good job of managing many of the other details of my life so I could write.

No book gets written without people who put in endless hours on behalf of the author. My heartfelt thanks goes out to all who helped me.

One thing more: In this book I relate stories of persons who have been part of my ministry over the years. In many of these cases it has been necessary to change names and places to protect the persons involved; the stories have been modified so that anonymity can be maintained. But I want to thank these brothers and sisters in Christ, for without their involvement in my life I would have little to write about.

Introduction

A FEW YEARS BACK I wrote a book entitled *Twenty Hot Potatoes Christians Are Afraid to Touch*. It sold better than any other book I have written. It has also caused me more trouble. In that book, I tried to deal with a variety of social issues the church too often evades because they are so controversial.

I believe a church that is unwilling to tackle the difficult problems that confront us becomes a church that is irrelevant to the real world in which we live. The questions I tried to address in *Twenty Hot Potatoes* were:

1. How do we answer the challenge of AIDS?
2. Why are so many people down on themselves (and what can they do about it)?
3. What about women preachers?
4. Can a mother of a preschool child have a career and not feel guilty (and where does Dad fit into it all)?
5. What do I do if I'm sexually starved?
6. Is television evangelism a waste of money?

7. Should we pull our kids out of the public school system?

8. Can rich people get into heaven (or, can a Christian own a BMW)?

9. Does Christianity have any good news for homosexuals?

10. Should preachers start preaching against sports?

11. Is hunting a sin?

12. When is it okay to tell the doctor to pull the plug?

13. Where does a single woman over thirty go to get rid of the loneliness?

14. Can Christians kill?

15. Are funerals a ripoff?

16. Is it okay to put your aging mother in the county home?

17. Is it ever okay for divorced Christians to remarry?

18. Is a lot of psychological counseling a waste of time?

19. What should you do if your grown-up children are making decisions that could ruin their lives?

20. Are evangelicals too pro-Israel?

I list those questions here because if you have not read that book you may wonder why I am not speaking to some of those important concerns in this one.

This particular book could justifiably be labeled as a sequel to *Twenty Hot Potatoes*. Since the first book's publication, new issues have arisen, some of which may prove to be even more important than the ones I dealt with previously.

Stephen Hunter tells us we are presently engaged in what he calls *the culture wars*. The controversial questions that have come to dominate discussion in religious circles threaten the existence of any unity that is left in Christendom, and they set Christians against Christians with such ferocity that we begin to wonder when the shooting will begin.

With this present atmosphere, the easiest and safest thing for me would have been to leave it to others to address these difficult issues. I am an evangelist, and my work and ministry are seriously threatened when I move into unsafe territory by publicly considering controversial issues. But I have decided to do so for a number of reasons.

First, true Christianity never plays it safe. It is full of daring and adventure. It takes risks, and it speaks out to the society in which it is set. To sacrifice relevancy for careerism cannot be the way of those who would be followers of the most controversial Man who ever lived. However, I suppose I would be less ready to address many of the concerns in this book if I heard other voices articulating the ideas I have tried to express here. But I have not.

There is today throughout Christendom a new caution evident among the spokespersons of evangelical Christianity. There is a fear that to speak out on such issues is to endanger one's ministry—and everybody seems to have a ministry these days. Everybody seems to be raising money for something, and that makes most of us reluctant to do anything that might diminish our supporters' giving or in any way undercut the support base of our ministries. It is not so much that evangelical leaders are silent on these controversial issues as it is that most of what is being said tends to be set forth in terms that are "politically correct" in evangelical circles.

Political correctness is usually thought to be something the liberals are into. But I think we evangelicals are the ones who invented the concept. Ever since I can remember, I knew that being acceptable in the evangelical community meant not only believing in the doctrines of the Apostles' Creed and the inerrancy of Scriptures so I could be welcomed as a brother in Christ, but also holding to all of those political and social views that evangelicals treated as having been ordained by God. Those views have traditionally been related more to the platforms of the conservative wing of the Republican Party than to the teachings of Scripture. In fact, it comes as a shock to some people to learn they are not one and the same.

I do not deem myself as either a liberal or a conservative in politics. When I am asked where I stand, I always ask in response, "On what issue?"

On some issues, I identify with what political and social conservatives are saying. And on other issues, I sound like a liberal. In this book, I will try to stand above both political parties as I endeavor to make judgments on issues according to the teachings of Scripture.

Second, I turned sixty this year, and I am getting too old to play the games I am expected to play in order to remain active on the speaking circuit. I know if I say certain things there will be some cancellations on my speaking itinerary. There will be those who do not want a controversial speaker at their convention or assembly. I understand and accept that, but I do not worry about it. There are more than enough good evangelists and spokespersons to fill in where I am canceled or not invited.

I have come to that point in my life where I have to put my ministry in the hands of the Lord. If He wants me to be heard, then He will make a way for that to happen. And if He wishes for me to fade into the woodwork and withdraw from the evangelical speaking circuit, I am willing to accept that too. I am just tired of playing the games that require me to have the correct knee-jerk reactions on every issue if I am to be welcomed in certain circles. In this book I will express my beliefs, and I will do my best to be faithful to God and to Scripture as I do so—and I'll let the chips fall where they may. I'm not afraid. I know I won't be alone in the midst of the sawdust.

Note to International Readers

AMERICA IS UNIQUE in many ways, but the social and cultural issues now confronting American Christians are also stirring the minds of Christians in other countries. What I have written in this book is as much related to observations I have made on visits to Canada, the United Kingdom, New Zealand, Australia, and Singapore as it is to those I have made in my travels across the United States. My reflections and conclusions will prove to be just as relevant for people in those places as they are for Americans.

There is renewal in the American church. And this new-found dynamism has given Christians a new boldness as they confront the pressing problems of society. They are no longer willing to accept the encroachment of secularism on their culture without a counterattack. They are no longer ready to remain reticent about their faith in a world of religious pluralism, and they now demand their legal right to be heard. They are not about to allow the abuses of the sexual revolution to destroy the familial values which they believe to be biblically based. Christians have begun to seize the social agenda, and they demand a hearing.

In their efforts to live out the imperative to change the world into the kingdom of God, Christians have learned to organize and to translate their convictions into political action. To their surprise, they have found that when they demand to be heard, they are able to exercise significant influence in congresses and parliaments. As a matter of fact, Christians are beginning to succeed in their lobbying efforts beyond their wildest expectations.

All of this is pretty heady stuff. Christians are not used to power. And, like all cohorts of the powerless who are suddenly able to flex their muscles, Christians have to learn to be careful lest they abuse their new-found social significance.

Christians are learning that the old simplistic answers that served them well when nobody was listening will no longer do. They are coming to recognize that they need to look at the controversial issues with a new sophistication and that they have a responsibility to understand all sides of the raging debates of the times. And they are painfully aware that they are not quite ready to meet such challenges.

Perhaps the most dangerous reality of our times is that the leaders of political parties are out to seduce Christians into an alliance with their particular partisan interests. They want to make the church a political block that can be delivered to the candidates of their choice. These politicians flatter us with their attention, and after having been ignored by them for so long, we are all to ready to fall for their flattery.

Suddenly, religious spokespersons have become media celebrities and are increasingly regular guests on television and radio talk shows.

On the one hand, this is a good thing because it gives us a chance to penetrate a secular society with our message. But on the other hand, this is a dangerous thing. As we become increasingly media conscious, we are apt to tailor and shape the gospel to meet the requisites of good broadcasting. And this, of course, can lead to a distortion of the gospel. It can also lead to Christianity's becoming just one more entertaining "bleep" on the television screens across the world.

All of these dangers are being faced by American Christians.

That is because it is here in the United States that evangelicalism has had its most dramatic success. But it is easy to find the same forces at work and the same dangers evident in other countries. Much that is happening in New Zealand, Australia, the United Kingdom, Canada, and in other countries looks very much like what is going on right here in my country.

That is why I believe that this book is relevant beyond the borders of the United States. The names, places, and political parties undoubtedly are different from other countries, but the issues, dangers, and concerns remain the same.

Readers who are not from the United States may have to do some "translating" to adapt some of this material to their own societal system. But in the end, I am sure that Christians everywhere will fully understand the issues this book examines. And I fear that if we do not handle these issues with grace, love, and wisdom, the church may find itself an early victim of our postmodern era.

1

Is Jesus a Republican
or a Democrat?

DURING THE SIXTIES, if you attended a mainline denominational church, you could easily come away believing that Jesus was a Democrat. The social-justice concerns of those churches seemed to mesh smoothly with the platform of the Democratic Party. The attacks on racism, poverty, and sexism that formed the core of the Democratic agenda were also primary concerns of mainline denominations.

At the annual assemblies and conventions of those denominations, debates focused on liberal social issues. Resolutions were passed that lent theological and biblical legitimation to the "progressive" ideals being championed by the Democrats.

Those were the days of Martin Luther King and his dreams for America. Those were the days when the support many conservative Christians gave to the war in Vietnam made them seem morally bankrupt, especially in the eyes of the under-thirty generation led by Bob Dylan. The temperament of the country was liberal, and the mainline denominations created for America a God who incarnated their liberal causes.

But now the pendulum has swung. Conservatism now appears to be the unstoppable social ideology. In both politics and religion (and it is often impossible to distinguish between them these days), the movement toward the right seems irresistible. The mainline churches with their social consciousness and their stellar liberal credentials find themselves in rapid decline. Nowadays, it is the new nondenomination superchurches with their highly individualistic way of salvation that have the momentum for growth. Theirs is a brand of evangelical Christianity that tends to embrace the conservative social agenda of the Republican Party, which has now become the primary force for molding the religious culture of our future.

Suddenly, it seems as though God has switched political affiliations. These days, God seems to have become a deity owned by the Republican Party.

Awhile back, George Bernard Shaw remarked, "God made man in His image, and we have decided to return the favor." Shaw, in his cynicism about religion, recognized the tendency of those in various political parties to define God as little more than a collective representative of themselves. Republicans may dress Jesus in a Brooks Brothers suit while Democrats put Him in the denim work clothes of union workers. Among those who espouse liberation theology, Jesus is usually portrayed as looking a lot like the late Cuban revolutionary Che Guevara.

There is no better way for a political party to establish the legitimacy of its political point of view than to declare that Jesus is one of its members. This remaking of Jesus is not just some kind of harmless campaign technique. It is not merely something sophisticated sociological observers can pass off with a wry smile and a wave of the hand. It is not just bad religion that needs correcting. *The Bible calls it idolatry!* The apostle Paul wrote:

> Professing themselves to be wise, they became fools, and changed the glory of the uncorruptible God into an image made like to corruptible man. . . . who changed the truth of God into a lie, and worshipped and served the creature more than the Creator, who is blessed forever. Amen. (Rom. 1:22–23, 25)

The apostle Paul saw in this a tendency for people to create for themselves a god who symbolized the political and economic interests of their own special interest group and who ordained the values of their own particular lifestyle. But the God revealed in Scripture is neither a Democrat nor a Republican.

The true God calls us away from such idolatrous tendencies. He stands above all political parties and calls each of them into judgment. Likewise, He calls upon us to rise above all of this, and He expects us to use the Scriptures as a touchstone to test whether the policies and practices of political parties are in harmony with His will. God expects us never to let partisan loyalty tempt us into reading the platform ideas of any party into the Bible. If we are to be faithful to the true God, we must not allow the principles of any party to override what the Bible has to say to us.

What I am saying is not a put-down of either major political party; each of them incorporates some of God's truth and emphasizes some of the good that God requires of us. For instance, I find that the Republican Party is biblically on target with its emphasis on individual responsibility. Republicans expect people not to blame others for problems that are the result of their own shortcomings and failures. Republicans come down especially hard on able-bodied men and women who unjustly collect welfare benefits. Those welfare recipients who ought to be working but who instead live off the labors of others are prime candidates for the righteous indignation of Republicans. America, Republicans claim, is a land of opportunity. Therefore, they usually view personal failure as the result of an individual's own shortcomings and lack of effort rather than as the consequence of social injustices such as discrimination and prejudice.

Democrats, on the other hand, are more likely to see the ways in which society can victimize people. Democrats are the ones who are likely to see how social structures can function unfairly to keep certain groups of people from being able to fully share in the American Dream. Democrats are the ones most committed to ending those policies or practices that deny to any ethnic, economic, or gender group the equal opportunities that a just society should provide for all of its citizens. It is the Democrats who seem more than ready to try to correct past injustices suffered by those who have been the victims of prejudices. Whereas the Republicans pick up the biblical emphasis on personal responsibility, the Democrats are big on trying to make government compassionate. It might even be said that each of these parties has a tendency to overemphasize these respective dimensions of the gospel.

Each of these parties has its strengths, but each of them also has weaknesses. Sometimes the rhetoric and attitudes of Republicans seem mean. Sometimes they fail to recognize that many individuals in this society cannot compete in our *laissez faire* economic system because they have been denied the chance to learn the skills and to develop the traits that make for social success. Some people who never really had a chance to succeed are labeled as losers.

Democrats, on the other hand, often tend to see big government as the answer to every social problem. They seem reluctant to admit there is anything wrong with society in general or with individuals in particular that government cannot correct. It almost seems as though no one can dream up a new government program the Democrats do not like.

Democrats often do not understand that, in the end, individual volunteerism encouraged by churches and civic groups (and not a host of new programs sponsored by Washington) is what is needed if we are going to solve the social problems that now overwhelm us.

Most of the needs of those who are marginalized and left behind in the American race toward success cannot be met by government. Instead, our churches need to inspire their people to reach out to those around them who have fallen between the cracks and become part of the growing underclass of America. Unless Christians recognize their responsibility to the less fortunate, little progress can be made toward alleviating the sufferings of the socially disinherited. The privileged must carry out their "noble obligation" toward the underprivileged on a personal, caring level if we are even to begin to rescue those among us who seem to be drowning in hopelessness and despair. To this end, the Bible reminds us: "For unto whomsoever much is given, of him shall be much required" (Luke 12:48b).

But even as we emphasize the Christian responsibility to the needy, we must know that the church by itself lacks the financial resources to meet all the needs of those who are in desperate straits. There is not enough money in the offering plate to care for the needs of those who, in the race for the American dream, fall by the wayside. And the Democrats are right in telling us that the government has a responsibility to help these unfortunate people.

Each party has its positives as well as its negatives. It has been said that the difference between a Republican and a Democrat is this: If someone is drowning one hundred yards offshore, the Republican will throw out fifty yards of rope and yell, "I've done my part; now it's time for you to do your part."

The Democrat, on the other hand, seeing someone drowning one hundred yards offshore, will throw out two hundred yards of rope and then drop his end.

I believe the Republicans are right in their strong emphasis on individual responsibility. There is no doubt that on Judgment Day each and every one of us will be held accountable for what we did and failed to do. On that great day, each of us will have to own up to the fact that much of what happened to us in this life was the result of our own decisions. And when it comes to salvation, we will be asked if we made that most important decision of all—the decision to accept or reject Christ. The Bible makes it clear that God has given to each of us the responsibility for making that ultimate decision about where we will spend eternity:

> But as many as received him, to them gave he power to become the sons of God, even to them that believe on his name. (John 1:12)

The word is nigh thee, even in thy mouth, and in thy
heart: that is, the word of faith, which we preach; that if
thou shalt confess with thy mouth the Lord Jesus, and
shalt believe in thine heart that God hath raised him
from the dead, thou shalt be saved. (Rom. 10:8b–9)

But if Republicans drive us to see the extent to which we must
accept personal responsibility for our personal destinies, the
Democrats make us aware that for many of us there are social circumstances that make us into sinners. It is quite possible for individuals who would otherwise be good people to be caught up
in social circumstances that make them sinners unconsciously.

Over the years, there have been many Christians who have
been loving and kind as individuals yet have unquestioningly and
supportively been part of a society that has practiced racial discrimination. As individuals, these people would never have diminished the dignity of another person, but they experienced no
guilt as they joined with others to create institutions and practices
that insulted and hurt huge numbers of people.

What the Democrats bring to our attention is the fact that
there is often unnoticed "structural evil" in society. Sometimes
there are social arrangements that are demonic in their effects
on people. The Democrats remind us that, if there is to be righteousness in the nation, we must do more than just hold each
other accountable for what we do as individuals. We must also
hold each other responsible for what we do collectively. We must
seek to do right both as persons and as a nation. Individually, we
are to yield to the leading of the Holy Spirit in our lives and become obedient servants of Christ who love one another. Collectively, we are to work together to change the social institutions of
our nation so that everyone enjoys justice and hope. Collectively,
we must join with Christ as He works in history to change the
kingdoms of this world into the kingdom of God.

Sometimes, when I am talking to Christians who are Republicans, I get the sense that they believe that all we need to create
a good society is to get individuals "saved." They seem to simplis-

tically believe that society is nothing more than the sum total of the individuals who make it up. Some Republicans lead me to believe that, to the extent we get people "saved," society will become what God wants it to be.

On the other hand, when I talk to Democrats who are Christians, I sometimes get the idea that all we have to do to make things good in America is to create a more just social order. Too often, Democrats convey the simplistic notion that the only reason people do evil is because society sets them up for it. To listen to some Democrats I know is to get the idea that if the government just ensured everyone of adequate housing, decent-paying jobs, and good educational opportunities, all would be well.

In reality, each side has half the truth. We will never have a good society unless individuals are personally transformed by the Holy Spirit. But neither will we have a good society if we do not address the structural evils we find in the social arrangements of our time.

Democrats have been guilty of nurturing a culture of victimization in which those who do not seem to be "making it" in America can too easily blame what "the establishment" has done to them rather than face up to their own personal failures. To illustrate what I am trying to express, allow me to tell you the story of Felesha. She is a young African-American woman who now is behind bars, having been caught in a drug bust. Selling drugs is an ugly thing to do, and Felesha must face the fact that she is personally responsible for the place in which she finds herself today. But there is more to her sin than willful disobedience to the commandments of God.

I first met Felesha when she was fourteen years old. She came regularly to a Bible-study club I had helped start in the government housing project where she lived. She had been born out of wedlock and had never met her father. Her mother, who was seventeen years old when she was born, had never held a steady job.

The school Felesha attended was one of those worn-out

buildings with walls covered with graffiti and trash strewn everywhere. The city's department of education had made Felesha's
campus the dumping ground for teachers who had caused problems in its better schools. Most of those who attended class with
Felesha were functionally illiterate, and no one seemed to care.
The school was designed to do only one thing—get the kids
through. Students were promoted whether or not they had
learned anything, and diplomas were handed out for nothing
more than showing up for school, more or less, for twelve years.

After being in our Bible-study club for a couple of months,
Felesha accepted Jesus as her personal Savior. She decided she
wanted to be a Christian, but there were some social situations
that would make being Christian more than she could handle.

Felesha's mother had a constant stream of "boyfriends" passing through her small, dilapidated apartment, and one night
while the mother was in an unconscious, drunken stupor, one of
the men raped Felesha. Nine months later Felesha gave birth to
a baby girl.

Felesha had feared that something like this was going to happen to her because the man who raped her had "come on to
her," as she said, several times earlier. He had even warned her
that sooner or later he was going to have her. When Felesha told
her mother about the threat, she got no support. There was no
loving family to protect her. She told the leader of her Bible-study
club what was going on, but there seemed to be nothing that
could be done. The social worker who supervised the family had
wrongly told Felesha that unless her mother was willing to file a
complaint, her hands were tied.

Felesha dropped out of school, but without any skills and being hardly able to read, she couldn't get a job. She had to move
out of her mother's apartment (which she very much *wanted* to
do) in order to be eligible for welfare benefits.

And so it was that Felesha, at the age of seventeen, was repeat-
ing the life of her mother. She was "saved" by the grace of God,
but she had become the victim of "principalities" and "powers"
beyond her control. There was her family, or what she consid-

ered to be a family, which had horribly failed her. There was her school, which had cheated her out of an education. There was the government's welfare system, which was tied up in so many bureaucratic rules it was unable to meet her needs. There was the HUD housing project where she lived, which because of government cutbacks lacked the maintenance funding that would have kept it from becoming a slum. And there was the social worker who was either misinformed or too lazy to help Felesha find a way out of an intolerable home situation. Given all of these overpowering "principalities" and "powers" demonizing her life, is it any wonder that Felesha's commitment to Christ crumbled and that she took up with the man next door who offered her a chance to make a few bucks selling crack?

Even so, Felesha is responsible for what she did, but so are the principalities and powers. In Ephesians 6:12 we read, "For we wrestle not against flesh and blood, but against principalities, against powers, against the rulers of the darkness of this world, against spiritual wickedness in high places."

To live out the Christian life, Felesha would have had to stand up to the temptations of the flesh, like getting sexually involved with the man next door, just to experience something that felt like love. It would also have involved struggling against social structures like her family, the educational system, the welfare system, and the government housing authority—all of which seemed to conspire to destroy her. These social structures are what Paul referred to as "principalities" and "powers." Felesha was defeated both because of her personal failures and because of the evil ways in which society and its institutions had failed her.

Republicans emphasize the personal responsibilities that should be assumed by people like Felesha. They want to create a government that would encourage such people to act responsibly.

Democrats, on the other hand, are constantly calling us to use the power of government to change the social structure so that it would serve people like Felesha justly. They believe the disadvantaged should be helped by special government programs.

They want to change America so that when people compete for success, they will play out the game on a level playing field.

Political conservatism has become so popular among evangelicals that they are prone to make being Christian synonymous with the Republican ideology. Almost all of the hundreds of Christian radio talk shows that seem to crowd the airways articulate the views of conservative Republican politics.

The Christian Coalition, which is the most organized expression of conservative religious politics, is so committed to the Republican Party's "Contract with America" that to many, this set of legislative proposals almost takes on the character of a religious document.

In the face of this growing commitment by evangelicals to conservative Republicanism, some of my friends have asked me how it is possible to be a Democrat and still be a Christian. In response to such an inquiry, I must admit to concerns I have about the platform of the Democratic Party that give me pause and force me to do some soul-searching. Indeed, there is much that Republicanism is about that seems in tune with the thrust of the Bible, but there are also a variety of concerns that keep me from being swept into the mind-set of those who believe that conservative Republicanism is the only way to go. In order to help my brothers and sisters in Christ to understand why I am not enthusiastic about the alliance that has grown up between evangelicalism and conservative Republicanism, let me explain myself.

First of all, I am not as trusting of big business as my Republican friends seem to be. As a case in point, I am concerned about the ways that drug companies jack up the prices of pharmaceuticals so that many poor people, particularly among the elderly, cannot afford to buy them. The markup on some medicines can be as much as a hundred times more than the cost of production. The fact that people suffering from diseases like AIDS have to pay exorbitant prices to get the medicine they need for survival seems horribly unjust. Actually, it is possible to go to other countries and purchase some pharmaceuticals much cheaper than they can be bought here in the United States, where they are produced.

But the drug companies are not the only big businesses I am convinced ought to be controlled. I am also alarmed over what the oil companies are doing to us. I cannot, for the life of me, figure out how we allowed them, as a means of optimizing their profits, to make us dependent on oil from the Middle East. The risky involvements and political responsibilities that such dependencies require make our economy subject to the whims of sheiks. All of this goes on while our own oil reserves in Texas are capped and left unused.

I could go on, but let it be said that I am not convinced that the government that governs least is always the government that governs best. I believe that the government has to exercise more control over such industries as oil for the public good.

My conservative friends applauded the massive deregulation of the economy that occurred during the Reagan-Bush era. But I, for one, was horrified when I found out that the removal of government control of the savings-and-loan industry led to abuses that cost the American people more than a trillion dollars and, for countless numbers of ordinary people, meant the loss of their life's savings.

While most conservatives think the government ought to stay out of the private sector, I want the government to make sure the corporate community does not continue to dump toxic waste in the indiscriminate ways that have been all too common in the past. I believe an unrestrained corporate America will devastate the environment in a host of ways as it seeks to optimize profits for shareholders.

I would like to believe that my conservative friends are right when they contend that racism and sexism are no longer factors influencing social practices in America. But I fear that without government directives and guidelines, discrimination will be omnipresent in the land. The maintenance of fair housing practices and equal opportunity in employment requires great vigilance by government.

While many Christian Republicans are decrying big government, I contend that the government has an obligation to step in and control the costs of healthcare. There is evidence that prices are set almost arbitrarily, so that a surgical operation can cost two thousand dollars or ten thousand dollars, depending on the hospital in which it is performed. Furthermore, the often unjustly high cost of medical insurance has resulted in millions of Americans being left uninsured.

Certainly, most citizens would agree that the legal profession needs to be brought under control. Even politically conservative Christians recognize that the time has come for government to regulate which cases can be brought to civil court and ensure that liability suits not be allowed to have crippling effects on persons, corporations, charitable organizations, and in some cases, even churches.

And finally, while my conservative friends condemn any curtailment of personal freedom, I believe that government must step in and limit freedom in certain areas. For instance, I do not believe that cigarette smoking should be allowed to continue when more than four hundred thousand deaths a year are linked to cigarettes and taxpayers have to pick up the bills for billions of dollars spent to combat smoking-related respiratory illness, heart disease, and cancer cases. I say that government ought to step in and tell smoking addicts that their freedom to pollute the air and to create huge problems for the rest of us is over.

The fact that government has been inefficient and ineffective in the past is not sufficient reason to move to the kind of *laissez faire* policies that my conservative friends advocate. Instead, we must make government better and seek through government to make America into a society where the rich corporate structures of the country do not ignore the needs of the rest of us. Christians must be ready to create the kind of government that brings justice to all.

Biblical justice requires a higher degree of accountability on the part of the rich and the powerful because what they do so dramatically impacts the lives of those who have less wealth and less power.

Having cited what lures me toward the Democratic Party, let me now lay out some things about the Republican Party that very much attract me. First, I agree with the Republicans that the old answers to social problems posed by political liberals during the sixties will not work. Then I say that we have to find new ways of doing things. Big government with its "top-down" programs is not going to be the primary means by which we can effectively respond to crime, premarital pregnancy, drug use, illiteracy, joblessness, divorce, alcoholism, child abuse, homelessness, and domestic violence. We need a new kind of politics that emphasizes localism.

When the Republicans call for a new kind of politics that invites people at the grass-roots level to begin to solve the problems evident in their own neighborhoods, they strike a chord that resonates not only in my heart but in the hearts of most Americans.

We need a new kind of politics that on the local level calls together churches, community organizations, indigenous leaders, and government officials. Local people working together can best understand and address the problems they encounter in their own neighborhoods.

I believe conservative Republicans understand this new kind of politics and are the ones most likely to allow the churches to be full partners in such neighborhood coalitions. It is not that government ought not to be involved in our struggles to deal with the social problems that seem to overwhelm us in the places where we live; it is the *way* it is involved.

The day when big, expensive programs to solve local problems are designed by government experts in Washington is over. I am calling for a new kind of politics that will give decision-making power back to neighborhood people. These are the people who can make the best sense out of what is happening on their streets and who can best figure out what needs to be done to make things right. This does not mean that government dollars are not needed; it is just that government cannot be the primary social problem solver.

The resources of government are certainly required to deal with the needs of the poor. Government involvement is essential if we are to develop many of the programs that are essential to ensure all of our citizens a share in the American dream. As much as the church might want to replace expensive government welfare programs with programs of its own, we have to face the fact that it does not have the financial resources to do what needs to be done. But churches leading a broad-based community involvement of people of all political persuasions and organizational involvements and concerns can partner with government to efficiently and inexpensively address societal needs in ways that big government alone never could.

The people in Washington learned long ago that the best and cheapest way to help the poor in Third World countries is in cooperation with what they call private voluntary organizations. In administrating foreign aid programs, it was quickly learned that by entering into cooperation with church-based missionary organizations such as World Vision, World Concern, World Relief, and Opportunities International, the government could get far more bang for their dollars than if they tried to do the job without such partnerships. For instance, Opportunities International, an evangelical PVO based in Oak Park, Illinois, has been involved in job creation for the poor in countries around the world. More than forty thousand jobs have been created for Third World citizens through this organization at a cost to the federal government that is laughably low compared with most programs coming out of Washington. Why not do in impoverished rural areas and in disadvantaged neighborhoods right here in our country what has worked so well overseas? Partnerships between government and the private sector can be the wave of the future. And if the Republicans are the ones most ready to shift power out of Washington and back to the local level then Americans ought to give them a round of applause.

Second, there is no doubt that the Republicans have offered America the best hope for wiping out the national debt. For these efforts, they have drawn an increasingly positive response, even from many of the people who will lose benefits if government programs are slashed in accord with Republican proposals. We all see something morally wrong with spending programs that benefit us while building an unbearable debt that will crush our children and grandchildren. Furthermore, Christians have biblical directives against debt and stand opposed to lifestyles that get people to live beyond their means. If a balanced budget is a Republican thing, then they are on to something that most Christians believe is part of the biblical ethic.

What you ought to have figured out from all that I am trying to say is that each political party has much for Christians to embrace. And each has much for Christians to criticize. The last thing we should do is to ally the church of Jesus Christ with either of them.

Recently, the Christian Coalition contributed more than a million dollars to the Republican Party to support the Contract with America. In so doing, they created the impression in the eyes of many that evangelical Christians are simply religious Republicans. I consider it a mistake to tie up evangelical Christianity with Republicanism in this way. Jesus is not a Republican!

To counteract the Christian Coalition, there is a newly organized group called the Interfaith Alliance. This organization is made up mostly of people from mainline denominations who espouse a liberal legislative agenda. The Interfaith Alliance took twenty-five thousand dollars from the Democratic Party to further its causes. This too was a mistake, because Jesus is not a Democrat either!

Instead of participating in this kind of polarizing politics, I think Christians should embrace the politics of Jesus, which is a ministry of reconciliation:

> And all things are of God, who hath reconciled us to himself by Jesus Christ, and hath given to us the ministry of reconciliation. (2 Cor. 5:18)

It is not so much that Christians of various stripes on the political spectrum ought to be looking for *common* ground as that they ought to be looking for *higher* ground. They ought to be bringing their churches together, regardless of the differences that exist between them in terms of theological and political beliefs, in order to commonly address the social needs of their communities. Coalitions of churches ought to be calling upon service clubs, educational institutions, tenant councils, business leaders, union leaders, local political leaders, and whomever else wants to join them, pledging to work together to deal with the crises that confront us in every urban neighborhood and rural village in America. We cannot allow political divisiveness to mar the possibility for a new kind of political coalition that holds the promise of a better tomorrow.

To those who think we have to think alike to work for the good of the kingdom of God, let me remind you of what Jesus said about all of this. In His day, when there were reports of people who were not followers of Jesus but who were committed to the same ministries to the needy that He was about, He said, in effect, "Those who are not against us are for us" (see Mark 9:38–41). If Christ could declare a common good among those outside of His party and theology, and if He could urge His disciples to recognize that such people were involved in a common cause for the kingdom, ought we not to do the same?

In Christ, said the apostle Paul, "There is neither Jew nor Greek, bond nor free, male nor female" (Gal. 3:28). I can only say that if Paul were among us today, he would probably add, "and there is neither Republican nor Democrat. All are one in Christ Jesus, and in the cause of kingdom building." This is the higher kind of politics that does honor to our Lord.

Both parties are partly right and partly wrong. I am glad we have a two-party system in this country. And I am glad that God belongs to neither of them.

2

Do Real Christians Smoke?

WHEN I WAS a boy I heard sermons against smoking. I was told that the body was the temple of the Holy Spirit (see 1 Corinthians 3:16) and that smoking was a defilement of that temple. Giving up smoking was an assumed behavioral change that went with conversion, and those who were born again often gave testimonies about how the Lord had delivered them from their addiction to tobacco.

During my college days, I learned to make fun of those condemnations of smoking that had been so much a part of my childhood thinking. Rules against smoking came to be relegated to petty legalisms, and in derision, I joined the chorus that sang that little ditty that went:

> *I don't smoke.*
> *And I don't dance.*
> *And I don't chew.*
> *And I don't go with girls who do.*

But all of that took place before the surgeon general of the United States began putting out reports on the effects of smoking. It was before any of us knew about the high probability that smoking causes cancer, heart disease, and a variety of respiratory ailments. It was before anybody had figured out that smoking is the likely killer of more than four hundred thousand people a year in the United States and may be responsible for as many as a couple of million deaths a year worldwide.

There are those who will say that smoking is a private matter and that if people want to kill themselves, it's their own business. Smokers, especially, talk like this. But what they have to learn is that smoking is everybody's business. It is the rest of us who have to help carry the enormous costs that society incurs because of smokers. Each year, billions of dollars are spent on hospital bills to take care of those with tobacco-related cancer, heart disease, and respiratory ailments. The rest of us have to pay billions in taxes annually for Medicare and Medicaid, just to nurse those who are sick from smoking. Health-insurance premiums have skyrocketed, and one of the reasons is because of the financial burden we all have to bear to provide coverage for smokers.

Smoking not only kills smokers; it kills those who hang around smokers. Inhaling the smoke exhaled by others can do just about as much damage to our bodies as would be done if we smoked the cigarette ourselves. This inhaling of "secondary smoke," as it is called, can have an especially devastating effect on children. The children of smokers can be victimized by it for life. Diseases like asthma can be traced to it, and there is growing evidence that secondary smoke can cause mental retardation.

When all of the consequences for nonsmokers are considered, it is hard to make a case for the claim that smoking is a private matter.

What is incredible is that with all of this growing evidence of the evils of smoking, I seldom hear any mention of it in sermons these days. If I pick up Christian magazines, from *Moody Monthly* to *Christianity Today*, it is unlikely that there will be any articles decrying the sinfulness of smoking. It seems like the church has given up condemning smoking as a sin just when the reason to do so is indisputable and the urgent need for such sermons has become abundantly clear.

Anti-smoking should be a part of the pro-life message of the church. One of our critics has remarked, "The problems with evangelical Christians is that they think that life begins at conception and ends with birth. They act as though life should be protected up until a child is born, and then after that—forget it!"

Smoking takes almost one-third as many lives as are wiped out by abortions, yet there is not even a suggestion that condemning smoking is about to become part of the pro-life agenda. If there is a concern to protect the unborn, then we ought to be concerned about how *smoking* affects the unborn. The surgeon general's office contends that the prenatal effects of smoking are devastating on the health and the future well-being of the developing child in the womb.

One of the reasons why we say so little about smoking is that too many Christians make their living off of the tobacco industry. In Bible Belt states like North Carolina, tens of thousands of evangelical Christians work in the mills that turn out cigarettes. In all probability, most of them even tithe the money they make by working in the tobacco industry.

The political candidates heralded by the Christian Coalition because of their pro-life stand and their deep Christian commitment are not about to stand up to the tobacco industry. The money from that industry helps finance their campaigns at election time, and most of their Christian voting constituency would not be all that happy about politicians who threaten their jobs or the jobs of their neighbors.

Another possible reason why almost nothing is said about smoking from the pulpit these days is because so many people in our congregations smoke. Most preachers do their best preaching when they condemn the sins of people who do not attend church. But we have a tendency to back off when it looks like our "prophetic" message might offend those who sit in the pews.

The fact is that today smoking is a common habit among those in our churches, and in most cases, cigarette smoking is not a practice that is ended simply by making a strong resolution. The truth is that cigarettes are addictive; smoking cigarettes can be as addictive as heroin. Breaking the habit requires much more than good intentions. The evil of the leaders of the tobacco industry is more dramatic when we learn that they are well aware that tobacco is addictive. I was shocked when I read in the newspapers that more than a decade ago the industry's secret laboratory studies had confirmed the addictive nature of cigarettes. Not only did industry leaders keep this horrendous news secret, which we might have expected them to do out of economic considerations, but at congressional hearings it has been alleged that they actually *added more* addictive ingredients to their cigarettes. They *wanted* people to be enslaved by their addictions because that would keep them buying tobacco products. Oh, what "good" people are willing to do when there are some dollars to be made.

One of the most heartbreaking evils of the tobacco industry is the way its advertising is aimed at teenagers. Using cartoon characters and sexy billboards, marketing executives target young people, knowing if they can get *kids* hooked on cigarettes, they will have created addicts who will nurse their habits for a lifetime and spend a small fortune doing it.

Just when I was thinking the cynical evil of tobacco companies could do nothing worse to teenagers, I discovered that one of the major companies had developed an advertising campaign designed to get young African-American females to buy a new cigarette being developed "just for them." It is as though these teenage women don't have enough problems, so far as the cigarette lords are concerned. They are targeted to become addicted to a drug that will ruin their health and the health of their children.

I know we Americans are supposed to be advocates of *laissez faire* capitalism, but I, for one, think the government ought to do something about all of this. Furthermore, I believe Christians should make the regulating of the tobacco industry a high priority on their political agenda. After all, if we are opposed to the legalizing of other addictive substances, then why are we willing to let the sale of cigarettes go unchallenged? Last year approximately eight thousand Americans died of overdoses of heroin while more than four hundred thousand died from diseases related to smoking. Come on now! Which of these drugs—heroin or tobacco—ought to be considered the most dangerous for us and our children?

Tobacco is a drug. We don't think of it that way because we've been conditioned to view smoking as socially acceptable. But in every sense, tobacco *is* a drug, and it is the drug with the most devastating effects of any drug out there on the market.

I work with an inner-city ministry called Urban Promise, which reaches out to teenagers and children in what *Time* magazine has called the most run-down city in America: Camden, New Jersey. Among those whom we have led into a Christian conversion is a young man I will call Rashed.

The young man's life has wonderfully changed under the ministry of the faithful youth workers who serve with Urban Promise. He has ended sexual involvement with the several teenage girls he had been dating. He attends church with faithful regularity. Rashed is doing well in school, and he is singing with our gospel choir. But there is one area of his life that has obviously remained untouched by the transforming works of the Holy Spirit. Rashed is still selling drugs on a neighborhood street corner.

"Hey, I don't take drugs," he assures me. "I just sell them. I got to make money somehow. There sure ain't no jobs around here!"

I tried to convince Rashed how wrong it is to sell drugs. I explained that not taking drugs himself was not enough for a Christian. "After all," I told him, "what you're doing is hurting other children of God."

Rashed's response was most intriguing. What he said forces all of us to do some serious reflection. "How come you're going so hard on me?" he said. "I've heard your talk on cigarettes and how they're drugs. Well, what about the people from our church who sell cigarettes at their store? If cigarettes are drugs, aren't *they* pushing drugs? What about all those Christians who have cigarette machines in their restaurants? The only difference between my drugs and their drugs is that my drugs are illegal and theirs are more dangerous."

It's hard to respond to that kind of logic. It forces me to ask myself if I really ought to define cigarettes as drugs. That sort of rhetoric makes other drugs seem not so bad by comparison. And I certainly do not want to do anything that could lessen the seriousness with which we view the other drugs that plague our society. But then maybe the problem is not my rhetoric but the fact that we do not seem to view cigarettes as the dangerous, addictive drug they really are. Once we do recognize that cigarettes are drugs, our churches will be able to develop Christian ministries especially for smokers. To stop smoking, people need more than an admonition from the pulpit.

The Seventh Day Adventist Church is the only denomination I know about that has designed and implemented a program to help smokers break the habit. Their program is modeled after the Twelve Step program of Alcoholics Anonymous. But they add to their message the help of a support group and a lot of encouragement. Other churches would do well to adopt the Seventh Day Adventist program, because they are the experts in the field. In the Seventh Day Adventist program of deliverance for smokers, participants are made aware that cigarettes are so addictive that only with the intervening help of the Lord can victory over tobacco be achieved.

The apostle Paul wrote in Ephesians 6:12 that in the pilgrimage to grow into what Christ wants us to be we must "wrestle against principalities, against powers, against the rulers of the darkness of this world, against spiritual wickedness in high places."

As we deal with the threats and evils that come against us from the tobacco industry, we are facing suprahuman demonic forces. On the societal level we have to struggle against such principalities and powers as the advertising that is seducing us into believing that cigarettes are glamorous and fun. Madison Avenue is being used by Satan to lead us into destruction. The horror is that as our government has limited the advertising of cigarettes on television those in the cigarette industry have reacted by spending their television advertising dollars in Third World countries. Among the poorest of the poor of the world, this evil industry is at work enslaving the already oppressed to that which makes for sickness and death. When it promotes smoking, the advertising industry has become a principality and power used by the Evil One. We must struggle against it.

The business and industrial structures provide dividends for stockholders (many of whom are Christian) while they bring disease and enslavement to millions; these forces are principalities and powers that we must oppose. And the political system that feeds on the funding and the votes that come from the tobacco lords is also a principality and power that we must challenge in the name of Christ.

We must come to realize that on the personal level there is a demonic force at work that is binding people to the law of sin and death through smoking. Smoking is not just a bad habit. It is a work of the Evil One that must be destroyed (see 1 John 3:8).

Jesus came into the world to set these captives free. And those who smoke must come to know this Liberator. The Holy Spirit, who continues Christ's work among us today, must be introduced into their lives. In the Spirit, smokers will find the power that will buttress their wills to stand against their often-overpowering longing for cigarettes. And by encouraging smokers in their spiritual warfare, the church can once again use its pulpits to help people understand that smoking is not just a nasty habit that is a concern of pharisaic legalists. Preachers must be ready and willing to define smoking for what it is—one of the most serious social and spiritual problems of our times.

Christians have an obligation to organize and put pressure on state and national legislators to pass more controls on smoking. In reality, smoking should be illegal. The only reason why smoking has not been outlawed is that there are billions of dollars of lobbying power supporting the tobacco industry. I don't want to sound like I am going soft on marijuana, but as serious a hazard as smoking grass has proven to be, smoking tobacco is even more dangerous. Having outlawed marijuana, the only conclusion we can reach is that our failure to outlaw cigarettes is purely because of the enormous power the tobacco industry can buy with all its money. Don't think young people do not recognize this fact. Their cynicism about the political-economic establishment is only enhanced as they recognize that what is right and wrong, according to our laws, is controlled by wealth and not by biblical values or any sense of goodness.

Unfortunately, money does most of the talking these days when it comes to influencing our society and the behavior of our people. As a case in point, recent studies show that if we passed a tax on cigarettes that increased their cost by just 10 percent, one out of fifteen college students who now smoke would quit. But don't expect those who make the laws to act in the near future. They know what the tobacco industry can do to help them, and worse, what it can do to anyone who bucks it.

Over against the money and influence of the tobacco industry, we must muster the moral influence of the church. We Christians should make smoking a pro-life issue. We should be organizing to support legislation that will curtail smoking. We should be using our pulpits to counteract what is being sold on billboards, in print, and through the sponsorships of sport events from stock-car races (the Winston 500, for example) to women's tennis (such as the Virginia Slims Tournaments).

It's time for churches to act more prophetically, to stand up to the tobacco industry instead of accepting huge gifts from it to support their seminaries and colleges. It's time for Christians to recognize what smoking really is instead of treating it as just a bad personal habit. It's time for all of us to put up a "No Smoking" sign over the entire nation. It's time to get serious about this horrendous evil.

3

Do Christians Promote
Gay-Bashing?

THIS WAS A dangerous chapter for me to write, because I run
the risk of being misunderstood. Some people in the Christian
community will deliberately misrepresent what I am trying to say
about the way the church should respond to the gay and lesbian
community. There are those who delight in the attention they get
when they make sensational accusations about Christian brothers and sisters. And if such accusations prove false, these people
seldom acknowledge that or assume any responsibility for the
damage they have done to the ministries of those whom they
have misrepresented.

Over the past couple of years, I have been denounced on
"Christian" radio shows for views I have never held on the subject
of homosexuality, and I have been quoted as having said things
about gays and lesbians that I have never said. I can only assume
that those who deliberately misconstrue what I say do so because
their own homophobia drives them to negate any message that
might generate loving empathy for suffering gay brothers and
lesbian sisters.

So, just for the record, allow me to say up front that I believe
that Romans 1:19–21 eliminates any biblical basis for homosexual

25

relationships that involve same-gender genital contact. This passage of Scripture, although a source of intensive disagreement among biblical scholars, has provided the grounds for a historical tradition in the church that considers even monogamous homosexual liaisons as sin. I am one who holds that tradition.

However, I am not about to put this practice into some kind of "super-sin" category. It does not warrant the special kind of condemnation that has become increasingly common in the Christian community. To listen to some notable voices in Christendom, one could get the impression that behavior that defies the traditional teachings of the church on homosexuality puts a person into some kind of special category of the supercondemned.

I have been appalled by Christian parents who, while willing to maintain loving relationships with children who are into everything from drugs to promiscuity, will shun the child who admits to being homosexual. I am shocked to hear of churches that excommunicate homosexuals who sin but welcome other kinds of sinners into their fellowship whether or not they repent.

I am convinced that the fixation of certain preachers who hit on homosexual sin week in and week out is sometimes more the result of their own hang-ups than the result of their claim to being faithful servants of God. Sometimes when I hear the vehemence in the antihomosexual rhetoric of such preachers, I wonder if the protesters "doth protest too much."

Having declared loud and clear that I believe the Bible does not allow room for Christians to get into homosexual relationships that involve genital contact, let me get on with my concerns about the sufferings that some in the church are causing those in the homosexual community. . . .

It was supposedly a gathering of Christians who had come together to discuss "family issues." But the meeting was specifically about doing something "to defend society from what homosexuals are trying to do to us."

The leader of the group said he was determined to "expose

the facts about the homosexual agenda and how gay and lesbians are trying to get our children into their lifestyle." With all the heat and intensity of an evangelist at the highest pitch of his message, he gave to his rapt audience what he claimed were authoritative statistics: "Seventeen percent of all gays ingest human feces, 29 percent of them urinate on their partners, and 37 percent of them engage in sadomasochism."

I had heard those so-called "facts" before. The Christian leader standing up front failed to mention that the "scientific study" from which they were taken is highly suspect among social scientists and was made by a psychologist who had been expelled from the American Psychological Association for a breach of ethics that involved lying.

His listeners, unaware of this omission, feverishly took notes. There were gasps of dismay. It was obvious that this man's little speech had been effective. When group members were asked to respond, one of them stood and said, "These filthy people are an abomination to God and must be wiped from the face of the earth!"

It wasn't just what he said that frightened me; it was the way in which he said it. There was an evil intensity about him and a viciousness in his voice. The others at the meeting were not disturbed. Instead, there was a general agreement among them as people mumbled, "Amen" and things like, "Why don't we get this kind of message from the pulpit of our church?"

The sad fact is that members of some churches I know about *would* hear that kind of thing from the pulpit. And it is being preached not only from pulpits but through the media as well. A mother who asked her ten-year-old boy where he had heard the things he was saying—that gays molest little boys—was told, "From the preacher on television."

I am not saying that we in the church have condoned violence against homosexual people. But there is little doubt in my mind that some things that have been said in the church in the name of preaching the gospel have been taken as permission by misguided people to do terrible and evil things to gay men and lesbian women.

Anti-gay rhetoric has long been a part of what is said from evangelical pulpits. At a "Jesus festival" that had brought together more than twenty thousand young people, I once had to follow a speaker who became a sensation as he whipped up animosity against homosexuals. He sent shivers of revulsion through the crowd with his vivid descriptions of what he claimed were common homosexual acts. His explicit details of sadomasochistic body mutilations and his generalizations about how homosexuals defecate on each other to get perverted thrills achieved the desired ends. Out of the crowd of young Christians, someone yelled, "Kill the fags!" The evangelist stopped and piously responded, "Oh no! We should love them! We must hate the sin, but we must love the sinner."

As I stood backstage, waiting to be the next speaker on the program, I wondered how that man out there figured he loved homosexuals. Was it love to exaggerate the facts and create a frenzy of hate among young people? Was it love to aggrandize his image as a sensational preacher at the expense of the homosexual teenagers who silently suffered as they listened to his tirade? Was it love that stirred some sick kid in the crowd to scream about killing "fags," sending fear into the hearts of every gay and lesbian teenager who had to listen to it all in silence? It is so easy to say, "We should love gays and lesbians," after having stirred a crowd to fear and hate them. It is harder to put that admonition into practice.

Donald Aldrich was the kind of disturbed and pathetic young man who responds to such inflammatory talk. One frigid night in November of 1993, Donald abducted a twenty-three-year-old gay man and later killed him. At gunpoint, he took Nicholas West to a dark and lonely gravel pit just outside of Tyler, Texas, and worked out some of his own religiously inspired hatred of gay people. By his own admission, Aldrich punched and kicked West into a bloody mess. He battered the face of this gay man by pistol-whipping him with a .357 magnum. Then he, along with his friends, pumped eight bullets into the dying man. They wanted to make sure he suffered, so they put some of the shots through his arms and hands before firing the final shot through the back of Nicholas West's head.

When Aldrich later confessed to police, he could not conceal a twisted smile of gratification as he talked about having so frightened West that the man had soiled his pants. Aldrich also revealed that in his own mind there was a religious legitimation for his merciless cruelty. *Vanity Fair* magazine reported what he said at his trial:

> They're doing something that God totally condemns in the Bible. But look at everything they've got. They've got all this nice stuff. They've got all these good jobs—sit back at a desk or sit back in an air-conditioned building not having to sweat, not having to bust their ass, and they've got money. . . . So, yeah, I resented that.

Poor Donald Aldrich! The transcript of his trial shows he was full of self-contempt and felt like a "nothing." He was one of those young men who, because they feel like losers, look for someone to blame. And instead of being led by the church to discover his preciousness as a child of God and his own potential in Jesus, Donald Aldrich had heard things that fed the cancer of his resentment. He was not nurtured into the fruits of the Spirit that would have given him "love, joy, peace, longsuffering, gentleness, goodness, faith, meekness, [and] temperance" (Gal. 5:22–23). Instead, the messages he heard from the pulpit had connected with destructive emotions that festered in his heart.

Anyone who knows history will recognize immediately what is going on here in the name of religion. This is not the first time a demagogue has played on the fears and resentments of those whose psyches are filled with self-contempt. Nor is it the first time those who feel cheated by life's chances and believe someone out there must be held responsible have eagerly embraced such a message. There have always been those who would rise to power by fanning the resentments of those who feel like "nobodies"— telling them that some evil group out there has covertly victimized them. Hitler did it in the 1930s, making the Jews the target of the hateful resentments eating away at the beaten-down German people. And if we study what Hitler did and said about Jews back then, we will be painfully aware that we are hearing something very close to it today.

The demagogues of our time have made homosexuals the new Jews, and now the call for persecution is made in the name of God. While there are Christians who will be outraged by this comparison, it should be noted that social scientists studying the gay-bashing phenomena have no trouble discerning that these are parallel situations.

The first thing we in the church must do to show our repentance for all of this is to commit ourselves to telling people the truth. For instance, the truth is that there *are* gay and lesbian perverts who threaten little children; but there are also heterosexual perverts who threaten little children. The truth is that, when we study the actual facts and figures, the proportion of the homosexuals in this country who molested children last year is the same, probably even a little lower, than the proportion of those in the heterosexual community who molested children. Sexually molesting children is a horrendous evil; the Bible says:

> But whoso shall offend one of these little ones which
> believe in me, it were better for him that a millstone
> were hanged about his neck, and that he were drowned
> in the depth of the sea. (Matt. 18:6)

But to declare from the pulpit that homosexuals are more likely to commit such a hideous crime than are heterosexuals is just an out-and-out lie. The amount of heterosexual molesting and incest that goes on in our society staggers the imagination. And considering the small number of homosexuals who ever commit this crime, we ought to recognize that heterosexual offenders should be our primary concern when it comes to protecting our children.

Second, those alarmist sermons that describe homosexuality as being on the rise across America are false. The accompanying declarations that most gays and lesbians are generally into the kind of filthy behavior that involves bodily wastes is a gross exaggeration designed only to inflame hatred. The most comprehensive sex study in recent years, made by researchers at the University of Chicago, states that only about 5 percent of men have homosexual desires, and only about half of them ever act out their desires. The statistical evidence clearly suggests that most homosexual men live very circumspect lives and seldom if ever have any same-gender physical relations.

One thing more: In most typical church services, there are probably gay and lesbian persons who have come to worship. In all probability, they are people who live decent lives. They are not into any of the kinds of disgusting orgies described in the demagogic preaching that too often comes from our pulpits. These men and women are likely to be living celibate lives in accord with what they believe Scripture requires of them. Most of them are still "in the closet" and live in fear that their sexual orientations will be discovered. All too often, because they have no one with whom to share their secret, they have to struggle alone against sexual temptation. What they do not need is for some fire-eating preacher to add to their suffering with stupid and mean remarks—all in the name of Jesus.

Let's face it! Nobody knows what causes homosexuality—it is probably the result of a combination of factors that interact with each other. To complicate matters more, the interplay of those factors is likely to take on a unique configuration for each and every person. Most researchers are convinced that the primary causes of homosexuality among men are different than the primary causal factors that make women into homosexuals. That is one reason why simplistic explanations given by those "pop" psychologists who are often guests on Christian radio shows have to be seriously questioned.

The followers of Sigmund Freud explain homosexuality among men as the result of boys having grown up without a strong father image. Given such a situation, say the Freudians, such boys are likely to make a poor identification with their fathers and instead, sexually identify with their mothers. The fact that most Christians deem Freudian theory as anti-Christian — and the additional fact that there is not one iota of empirical evidence to back up Freud's claim — does not keep evangelicals from making the Freudian explanation the one most commonly accepted in their circles.

It should be noted that Freud's explanation of the causes of homosexuality had an entirely different bent when he dealt with lesbian women. According to Freud, in the psychosexual development of the female, the erogenous zones change, and if the female, because of failures to properly mature, becomes "fixated" prior to her vaginal tract becoming her primary erogenous zone, the result will be a homosexual orientation. Once again, there is absolutely no evidence to support this theory, and it stirs a lot of anger among lesbian women who resent being defined as persons who would want sex with men if they would just "grow up."

A more recent psychotherapeutic theory is outlined by two theorists who have become very popular in some evangelical Christian circles. This is a theory connected with the "reparative therapy" being promoted by Elizabeth Moberly and Joseph Nicolosi. One should not assume that Moberly and Nicolosi are colleagues. They are anything but! Moberly contends Nicolosi "stole" her theory, is taking all the credit, and is making a lot of money from it. I do not know the truth about the first part of that accusation, but there is little doubt about the second part. Nicolosi has become very popular with those homosexuals who are looking for someone to help them change their sexual orientation. In a *Time* magazine account of Nicolosi's work, it was noted that while he had just a few cases to offer as examples, those few men spoke in glowing terms about the success of reparative therapy.

On the other hand, to date, I have been unable to interview or even get the names of clients that Moberly says she has helped. She claims "professional confidentiality" as the reason her clients remain anonymous.

The Moberly/Nicolosi theory put a different twist on Freud. While in agreement with Freud that relationships with parents lie at the bottom of the problem, Moberly and Nicolosi go on to claim that homosexuality is caused when a child has trouble relating to his or her parent of the same sex. In short, it is because of conflicts and deprivations that occur in a girl's relationship with her mother or a boy's relationship with his father that homosexuality is created.

The problems I have with such psychotherapeutic theories lie, not only in the scarcity of scientific evidence available to support them, but in the fact that they end up placing the blame on parents. Parents go through enough agony trying to work through all that goes with having a homosexual child without some unsubstantiated theory adding to their pain by suggesting it is their fault. It would be a good thing for all Christians to recognize that, unless there is real evidence to justify such theoretical claims, they ought not to be used to lay guilt trips on people.

Most up-to-date findings confirm that in animals (and it is important to recognize that humans are different from and more than animals), sexual orientation is controlled by biological factors—specifically by hormones. Research done by many scientists shows that when there is a disruption of certain hormones at a crucial stage in the development of the fetus, the sexual orientation of rats can be significantly altered. Such disruption might be caused by some trauma or intense nervous tension in the mother during her pregnancy. The research suggests that sexual orientation is the result of programming or "imprinting" the brain of the rat fetus, and that the upset experienced by the mother can mess up this process, resulting in the homosexual orientation of her offspring.

When we come to humans, it is difficult if not impossible to get the kind of evidence we need to make assertions one way or the other about the influence of biological factors on homosexual orientations.

More recently, there have been some causal theories that attribute the cause of homosexuality to genetic factors. A recent study made at the Salk Institute noted the difference in the sizes of the hypothalamus glands in the brains of homosexuals when compared to the size of that gland in heterosexuals. The hypothalamus gland, which is the gland that controls sexual behavior, was noticeably smaller in the brains of homosexual men. In shape and size, the glands of the homosexual men resembled those of females. This study has been criticized because the glands of the homosexual men studied all came from men who had died of AIDS. More research in this area is needed and will undoubtedly be forthcoming.

Those whom I consider the experts in the field of study that deals with homosexuality contend that there is probably a multiplicity of factors that come together to establish the effect. What complicates things more, they argue, is that these factors interact in different ways and to different degrees in different individuals. All of this leads me to the obvious conclusion that those "easy to understand" explanations of homosexuality that are heard on some religious radio talk shows are oversimplifications that simply are not true.

Perhaps of more serious consequence is the fact that there is no simple "out" from a homosexual orientation. Those who suggest there are some "surefire" counseling techniques guaranteed to change a person's sexual orientation are probably offering false hope to those who would like to change. Sadly, I have to say that not even religious conversion offers a sure solution for the homosexual who wants to be "straight." Most gays and lesbians who become Christians and join evangelical churches enter into a lifelong struggle to live the kind of celibate lives that most of us believe are biblically required for them.

So many homosexuals who have sought to change their sexual orientation through religious means have ended up not only disillusioned but convinced that somehow God despises them in a special way. They have heard from the pulpit that God regards homosexuals as a special abomination and that if they would get right with God they would be free from homosexual temptation. After giving themselves over to God in every way they can, pleading in agony for God to change them, they are left to conclude that they have been predestined for damnation. The spiritual and psychological despair that follows is often more than they can bear.

Suicide is now the second major cause of death among teenagers, and according to one report, many of those suicides are committed by youngsters who despise themselves because of self-contempt due to their sexual orientation. I don't know everything the church should be about these days, but we certainly should not be about creating the despair that leads to self-destruction.

I am not saying God cannot change people from being homosexuals into being heterosexuals. *God can do anything!* I am only claiming that empirically we find that the overwhelming number of those who have sought "deliverance" through faith commitments have found that after all is said and done, their sexual orientation remains the same.

Some of my evangelical friends refuse even to consider the empirical evidence. They want to believe that if homosexuals will only repent and seek counseling, all will be well. They just don't get it. People can repent of what they do, but they cannot repent of who they are. Being homosexual is not just a bad habit that can be broken. It is an essential part of the identity of some of our brothers and sisters.

Those who ignore the empirical evidence often do so in the belief that homosexuals actually *decide* to be homosexual, or they believe homosexuals are "messed up" because they were molested as children. Such conclusions allow them to believe that all homosexuals can be changed and therefore are "guilty" if they accept their homosexual orientation rather than become involved in some kind of spiritually therapeutic cure process. If these people would only talk to enough homosexuals over extended periods of time, they would realize how hard most of them have tried and prayed and sought counseling—to no avail when it came to changing their sexual orientation. However, I have made it clear to the gay and lesbian people I have counseled that while they did not choose their sexual *orientation*, they do choose their *behavior*. And I let them know that I personally believe the Bible does not allow for same-gender physical sexual relationships.

What I hope for is more understanding for homosexuals from the rest of the Christian community. I want gays and lesbians to find in the church fellow Christians ready to support them as they come to terms with their sexual orientation and struggle daily to overcome the temptations they must face.

Personally, I look forward to a time when the church will have learned to respond to homosexuals in the same way we respond to alcoholics. There are many who do not like my making this comparison because it implies that homosexuality is a sickness. They have a point; but for the sake of my argument, allow me to continue in this line of thought.

There was a time when we assumed that alcoholism could be overcome simply by religious conversion. We expected alcoholics to be able to stand up at testimony meetings in church and say something like this:

> I was once an alcoholic. But then Jesus saved me, and since that day I have never had any desire for drink. The Lord took away all my craving for that cursed brew, and now I am completely free.

Undoubtedly, there are a few people who *can* give testimonies just like this. As a matter of fact, Glen Campbell, the well-known singer, claims such a miraculous healing and has told his story often on network-television talk shows. However, what is far more often the case is that the alcoholic who wants to stay sober is in for a daily struggle against temptation for the rest of his or her life. Nowadays a converted alcoholic in a supportive Christian community usually has a testimony that goes something like this:

> I *am* an alcoholic! I haven't had anything to drink for a long while. But the desire for drink is always with me, and I have to win the struggle against the temptation one day at a time. I want you to know that I am not alone in my struggle. I depend on a Higher Power, and there are also brothers and sisters who pray for me and are there for me in my times of dire need. Without them to support me, I would never make it. This is not a struggle that anyone can win on his or her own.

In parallel fashion, I am hoping that someday the church will allow a person who is homosexual to say:

> I *am* a homosexual! Since I gave my life to Christ I have not committed the kind of homosexual acts the Bible forbids. But every day I have to fight the battle against temptation over again. I want to thank God for the strength He gives me in this daily struggle, and I also thank God for the help of Christian friends. If it were not for my Christian brothers and sisters praying for me and upholding me, I wouldn't be able to make it.

We, the people of God, should be able to offer this kind of support to gays and lesbians who are part of our church fellowship. We are admonished to "bear one another's burdens" in order to "fulfil the law of Christ" (Gal. 6:2).

Conversion to Christ and membership in the body does not mean a person will not experience temptation anymore. It only means that, with the help of the Lord and the strength derived from Christian fellowship, he or she can be "more than a conqueror" (Rom. 8:37).

Right now we are a far cry from sympatheticly undergirding homosexual Christians who have chosen to be celibate out of devotion to Christ. The reality is that the evangelical community is, for the most part, opposed to any such suggestion. When President Clinton tried to change things so homosexuals in the military would not have to conceal their sexual identity to remain in good standing, there was an outcry in most evangelical churches. They wanted no part of a system wherein gays and lesbians could tell the truth about who they were and still remain in uniform. And yet, without that truth, there can be little hope and few victories.

I really don't know what we evangelicals think we have to gain by forcing gays and lesbians in the military to conceal their identity. There is no question that they are already there. Estimates of how many homosexuals are in the military exceed twenty thousand. Do we Christians want these hurting people to have to lie to evade court-martial? And if we want to win them to Christ, do we not have to create a social environment in which they can be honest about who they are?

We cannot have the kind of meaningful dialogue that leads to conversion unless those we witness to can be open to us and allow themselves to be vulnerable. When gays and lesbians have to conceal their true identities to keep their commissions in the military, hold jobs in the school system, and escape residential discrimination, it is not possible to minister to their real needs.

These are realities that all evangelicals will have to think through if they are to escape the label of homophobia that is all too often applied to them. The day of simple answers to the complex problems surrounding homosexuality is gone forever. All evangelicals must ask themselves if they have realistic good news for gays and lesbians who want to follow the Lord and be members of their churches.

4

Are Christian
Talk Shows Christian?

AN ANALYSIS of the 1994 election gave evidence that Christian radio had become a powerful force in America. A report in *USA Today* indicated that more than 37 percent of the voters cited radio talk shows as a major influence in determining how they voted. A great deal of that "talk radio" is on the Christian talk shows that now seem to be constantly available on the thousands of Christian stations across the country.

That Christian radio is a powerful influence in this country is abundantly clear. But more and more, questions are being raised about it, and more and more, there is evidence that it may be doing the cause of Christ a lot of harm. Some people are even asking if Christian radio is really Christian.

First of all, Christian radio seems to be overly biased in favor of the agenda of conservative Republicanism. It is not just that Christian radio talk shows express strong identification with the pro-life stand of conservative Republicanism; it is that they tend to be committed to the whole social philosophy of the Grand Old Party. The talk on these shows often portrays everything from foreign affairs to the domestic economic policy of the Republican Party as though it were ordained by

God. At times the listener can easily get the idea that God is a Republican.

There is nothing wrong with people examining the programs of political parties in light of Scripture and then concluding that one particular party or another embodies more perfectly the principles of God's Word. Nor is it wrong for a talk show host or hostess to go on the air to openly campaign for that party and explain to the listeners how, in his or her opinion, the truths of Scripture and the platform of that party harmonize. What *is* wrong is doing this overtly political campaigning as though it were the proclamation of the gospel.

As Americans, we are able to deduct the financial contributions we make for religious causes from our taxable income. But we are *not* allowed to take tax deductions for financial contributions we make for political purposes. Gifts to help elect particular candidates or to promote particular political parties cannot be considered as gifts to charity and thus are not allowed to be exempted as charitable gifts. But that *is* exactly what is happening across the country. Radio talk show hosts portray themselves as being involved in nonpartisan Christian ministries and ask for gifts that the givers write off as charitable gifts. Yet many of these talk show hosts are very much into partisan politics, and in not too subtle ways they endorse those candidates whom they believe best stand for Christian principles. That is both illegal and morally wrong.

A few years ago, the Federal Communications Commission did away with the Fairness Doctrine, a regulation that guaranteed equal time to opposing points of view on noncommercial programs. I am really sorry about that, because there is diminishing fairness and balance in what I now hear on religious radio shows. What comes across the air waves is often biased and partisan, and it ought not to be considered as religious programming at all. But it is. Christian radio, this incredibly influential instrument for forming public opinion, often implies and sometimes suggests that to be a Democrat is to be out of the will of God at best and perhaps is even enough to disqualify those who call themselves Democrats from membership in the family of God. Those broadcasters who avoid these tendencies ought to be applauded and encouraged because they are in danger of becoming a rare, if not extinct, breed.

Recently, I had the privilege of speaking at a governor's prayer breakfast. The governor, who was Republican, seemed to me to be a good example of how Christians can serve God in the political arena. I greatly admired him.

Following the prayer breakfast, the governor and I joined a group of high school and college young people to lead a discussion about Christians in politics. The first question asked was, "How could a person really be a Christian and be a Democrat at the same time?" The governor, to his credit, tried to explain to the young man who had asked the question that some of the most committed Christians he knew were Democrats. He went on to explain how different Christians worked out their convictions in different ways, and that while there was room for differing with others, there was no room for condemning them on the basis of the political party to which they belonged.

But the young man would have none of it. He told us the Christians he had heard on radio and television shows had made it clear to him that true Christians would not vote Democratic.

It is obvious from such responses that we have a problem here. It is a corruption of the intent of the law for religious broadcasters to get away with partisan politicking while still holding on to their tax-exempt status as religious ministries. But it is happening all the time.

The second problem I have with much of what goes out over the air from religious talk shows is that it is not always true. Granted, we need to leave room for honest mistakes, especially when those who make them are willing to admit their mistakes and set the record straight. But what do we say about those who deliberately lie because they are out to curtail the ministries or the careers of people they do not like?

There are some religious broadcasters out in the Midwest who are particularly upset with me because of my deep commitment to ministry to brothers and sisters suffering from AIDS. They see me as a mild deterrent to their attempt to designate AIDS as a special punishment from God on certain people whom they deem to be especially abhorrent to Him. In an effort to negate any influence I might have among their listeners, they have twisted and distorted what I have said and written over the years. Their aim is to discredit me as a bona fide evangelical and to take me off the Christian speaking circuit.

In one case, a broadcaster regularly tells his audience he is reading passages from my books. He then proceeds to make up things that most Christians would definitely consider heretical and morally outrageous. In at least one case, he claimed to be reading from page 422 of one of my books, when the book in question had only 228 pages! When I tried to personally visit him with the idea of working toward correction and reconciliation, I was told such a meeting would not be possible.

Another attack came from a broadcaster in Seattle, Washington, who said on his talk show and printed in his newsletter the following account of my preaching:

> Campolo says that Christ dwells in everyone, that going to heaven is like going to Philadelphia. . . . There are many ways. . . . It doesn't make any difference how we go there. We all end up in the same place.

If this were really what I had said or written, there would be justification for some of the accusations being made against me these days. But what I really said, as recorded in *World Vision* magazine (October/November 1988) was:

> It was one o'clock in the morning when I boarded the red-eye flight going from California to Philadelphia. I was looking forward to getting some rest, but the guy next to me wanted to talk.

"What's your name?" he asked.

I said, "Tony Campolo."

'And then he asked, "What do you do?"

Now when I want to talk, I say I'm a sociologist. And they say, "Oh, that's interesting." But if I really want to shut someone up, I say I'm a Baptist evangelist. Generally that does it.

"I'm a Baptist evangelist," I said.

"Do you know what I believe?" he asked. I could hardly wait. "I believe that going to heaven is like going to Philadelphia."

I certainly hope not, I thought.

"There are many ways to get to Philadelphia," he continued. "Some go by airplane. Some go by train. Some go by bus. Some drive by automobile. It doesn't make any difference how we go there. We all end up in the same place."

"Profound," I said, and went to sleep.

As we started descending into Philadelphia, the place was fogged in. The wind was blowing, the rain was beating on the plane, and everyone looked nervous and tight. As we were circling in the fog, I turned to the theological expert on my right. "I'm certainly glad the pilot doesn't agree with your theology," I said.

"What do you mean?" he asked.

"The people in the control booth are giving instructions to the pilot: 'Coming north by northwest, three degrees, you're on beam, you're on beam, don't deviate from beam.' I'm glad the pilot's not saying, 'There are many ways into the airport. There are many approaches we can take.' I'm glad he is saying, 'There's only one way we can land this plane, and I'm going to stay with it.'"

There is no other name whereby we can be saved except the name of Jesus.

Such lies and distortions have taken their toll on the ministries with which I am associated. Over the years, I have developed missionary work that ministers to some of the basic needs of children in Third World countries like Haiti and in urban ghettos here in the United States. What these religious broadcast-ers have been doing has led some of our supporters to cut off their giving. They have even been able to turn some young people away from coming to serve in our missionary endeavors.

However, anything these dishonest broadcasters have done to me is minor compared to what they have done to others in Chris-tian ministry. In the case of one of the more prominent and ef-fective evangelical ministries in America, the results of such lying and distortions have all but closed down the work. All of this ful-fills the pronouncements of James when he wrote: "Out of the same mouth proceedeth blessing and cursing. My brethren, these things ought not so to be" (James 3:10).

There really are no good viable options for dealing with the kinds of evil distortion that come from religious radio talk shows. The people involved are not willing to submit themselves to the kind of arbitration offered by such groups as the Christian Legal Society. And as Christians, those of us who feel unjustly treated are reluctant to go through the regular judicial system and sue such detractors for slander.

What really should be done is not being done. And that is that religious broadcasters themselves should work to keep each other ethical and fair. The National Religious Broadcasters should have a code of ethics and a set of broadcasting standards. They should also have a standing committee to review grievances and hand down judgments. Those who violate the code of ethi-cal practices or refuse to make corrections and restitution should be put out of the membership of the NRB. There should be a concerted effort by the NRB to set things right with anyone who has been hurt by one of its members.

I suppose the thing that bothers me most about religious ra-dio talk shows is that they are more modeled after the style of Rush Limbaugh and Howard Stern than any distinctly Christian standard. Caustic humor and ridicule is common in what they send out to their millions of listeners. Many of these hosts have become enamored with the fame of being entertainers. They seem to care little for the consequences of what they say, as long as they get a laugh or come across as being clever.

Most Christian radio talk show hosts and hostesses lack the time to research the claims they make on their shows. In almost every case, they do their programming without the kind of staff that responsible radio journalism requires. Consequently, there is a constant passing on of what they have heard from each other, without much checking being done to determine whether it is true. Their talk, all too often, is little more than sarcastic put-downs of people whose politics they despise. And too often, there is little concern for the damage their words may do to people.

Recently, I talked with a deeply committed evangelical Christian who once ran for the office of mayor in a major American city. Because he ran as a Democrat, the local religious radio talk show hosts made many false assumptions about him. They assumed he was pro-choice when in reality he was pro-life. They regularly depicted him as nothing more than an extension of the politics of President Clinton, when in reality there were major differences between him and the president. Even worse, these talk show hosts regularly called into question the sincerity of this good man and raised serious doubts as to whether he was really a Christian.

This man did his best to correct the erroneous reports about him. But when he tried calling the radio talkshow hosts and hostesses to ask them to set the record straight, his phone calls were not returned, and the false reports continued unabated. Little by little it dawned on him that these religious broadcasters were not really interested in the truth. They had many listeners who loved what they were saying, some who even considered them to be brave prophets. Many of them were becoming heroes in evangelical circles, and some had become popular speakers in the churches of the city. With "success" like that they were not about to let what happened to the victim of their malicious talk interfere with their budding careers. They came across as bright and witty, and that was what was important to them.

There is nothing wrong with Christians being entertaining. Quite the opposite, I think it is a good thing. But we have to be extremely careful about what we say, especially if we are naming names and accusing specific people of serious things. Paul said in 2 Corinthians 4:2:

> But [we] have renounced the hidden things of dishonesty, not walking in craftiness, nor handling the word of God deceitfully; but by manifestation of the truth commending ourselves to every man's conscience in the sight of God.

Beware of those who, for a cheap laugh or a clever barb, betray the gospel and twist the message of Christ for their own purposes. Society at large does not know what to make of it when people in one breath talk about the love of God and then, with the next breath, say things that are evil. James warned against such persons:

> But the tongue can no man tame; then it is an unruly evil, full of deadly poison.
> Therewith bless we God, even the Father; and therewith curse we men, which are made after the similitude of God.
> Out of the same mouth proceedeth blessing and cursing. My brethren, these things ought not so to be. . . .
> But if ye have bitter envying and strife in your hearts, glory not, and lie not against the truth.
> (James 3:8–10, 14)

There is a need for responsible Christian commentary on radio and television. But in our broadcasting, there is a need to measure up to the expectations of Scriptures, which are:

> Finally, brethren, whatsoever things are true, whatsoever things are honest, whatsoever things are just, whatsoever things are pure, whatsoever things are lovely,

whatsoever things are of good report; if there be any
virtue, and if there be any praise, think on these things.
(Phil. 4:8)

There is something good about getting a Christian perspective on the events of the day. We have turned toward Christian
radio and television talk show commentators, expecting them to
provide that for us. But they have, for the most part, let us down.
They promised us an alternative to what they called the liberal
biases of the secular press. But what they have given us in all too
many instances is their own biased perspective. In making their
case, they become careless with the truth and even, when it serves
their purposes, resort to slander.

There is a lot wrong with secular news reporting and commentary. But before we look for the splinters in the eyes of secular commentators, those responsible for Christian radio and
television talk shows had better get rid of the beams in their
own eyes.

5

What Should We
Do with Illegal Aliens, or
Is Proposition 187 Christian?

JOSÉ LOPEZ isn't supposed to be here. He's an illegal immigrant from Mexico. He and his wife and their three children sneaked across the border from Mexico in the still of the night. The crossing was easy. The porous border that separates the United States from Mexico is easily penetrated by those who long for a better life in the richest country on the face of the earth. And José was one of them.

The temptation was just too much to resist. Living in a shack patched together from odds and ends of cardboard, lumber, and corrugated-tin roofing he had scavenged from the nearby dump, this citizen of Tijuana knew there was a promised land of milk and honey just a few miles away.

"Up north," he said to himself, "there are jobs picking lettuce. My cousin Raphael went up there and got one of them. Now he can take care of his family. But look at me. I can't even buy milk for my children."

He asked himself, "Would God be angry with me just because I do what I have to do to take care of my family? Did not the evangelist from San Diego read to us from his Bible and say, 'He who does not care for his own family is worse than a heathen?' All I want for my family is a chance. I will work hard. I will be a good man. I will not make trouble for anybody."

José is glad he came. Even though he knows the farm boss for whom he works pays him way less than the minimum wage, he also knows it is better than the "nothing" he was earning back in Mexico.

José's wife does housework for a rich lawyer in San Diego. The lawyer is separated from her husband, and she needs José's wife not only to clean her house, but also to care for her two children. The twenty dollars a day she pays José's wife seems like a fortune to these illegal immigrants.

But now José wants more. He's thinking it would be a good thing for his daughter to go to school. And he, himself, may need some medical help. He has been coughing a lot, and some of the other pickers he works with are telling him he should see a doctor. But José is afraid to send his little girl, Rosita, to school because he has heard that the teachers there will report her and the police will come and arrest them for being illegal aliens. He is afraid to go to the local health clinic because he has heard that anybody who shows up at the clinic "without papers" will be reported to the immigration authorities.

The truth is that neither of these things is likely to happen because most teachers and doctors have more compassion than that. While they might be opposed to the illegal border crossings that have allowed families like José's to sneak into California, they probably will not turn their backs on people who are in need. But José doesn't know that. What he does know is that the other pickers are all talking about a law, Proposition 187, that the people in California voted for in the 1994 election. It is the proposition that would deny social services to illegal aliens like José and would require that those who apply for such services be reported to the U.S. Immigration Service.

Proposition 187 is the first such voter referendum passed in this country, but it is not likely to be the last. Arizona, Florida, Illinois, New York, and Texas are all considering similar action.

In Florida, citizens have formed a lobbying group called Floridians for Immigration Reform to make sure the state legislature takes whatever action is necessary to keep out those who have no right to land their makeshift boats on Florida's shores.

Most of us can figure out the reasons why the American public is ticked off by the huge number of illegal immigrants who have sneaked into our country, and especially why the citizens of California should be so upset. During the last decade, more than 3.5 million illegal immigrants from Mexico and elsewhere have slipped into the United States, and about 40 percent of them have settled in the Golden State. We have to spend more than eight billion dollars annually to aid these illegal immigrants, and half of that is paid by states that have no legal means to deny their services and no means to control the influx of illegal immigrants. It is easy to argue that these illegal aliens are not only breaking the law but that they are also an incredible financial drain on the American people.

Another reason to get tough with illegal immigrants is that there is a serious question as to how many new people this country can absorb in any given year without running into more problems than it can handle. If we add to the number of illegal immigrants the more than double their number who enter this country legally, we find we are adding about a million persons to our population every year. Can we find enough jobs, build enough housing, and provide enough social services for so many new citizens annually? Ina Melman of the Federation for American Immigration Reform based in Washington, D.C., has said that the time has come for tighter limits on how many people we should let come to this country.

But there's another side to all of this. It has to do with what is conscionable. There are secular spokespersons who contend there are moral considerations that cannot be ignored. And there are certainly those in the Christian community who believe there are also scriptural reasons why the hard line taken by initiatives like Proposition 187 is wrong. Charles Wheeler, the executive director of the National Center on Immigration Rights, has said, "We like to boast about how immigrants have built this country. Then we let racism and xenophobia lead us into saying things against them." Wheeler and others wonder if there would be such an uproar against aliens if they were white Anglo-Saxon Protestants instead of brown-skinned Latinos and blacks from Haiti?

Furthermore, when it comes to morality, a serious question can be raised as to how wrong it can be for Mexican people to emigrate to land we stole from Mexico just a hundred or so years ago. As one commentator sarcastically commented, "They have no right to live on land that we stole from them fair and square!"

Regardless of the arguments they come up with in secular society, those of us in the church have another set of considerations. Consider the fact that the Bible very specifically tells us we have a responsibility to the aliens who become our neighbors. For instance, Exodus 22:21–23 says:

> Thou shalt neither vex a stranger, nor oppress him: for ye were strangers in the land of Egypt.
> Ye shall not afflict any widow, or fatherless child.
> If thou afflict them any wise, and they cry at all unto me, I will surely hear their cry.

And then there's this in Leviticus 25:35:

> And if thy brother be waxen poor, and fallen in decay with thee; then thou shalt relieve him: yea, though he be a stranger, or a sojourner; that he may live with thee.

I could go on citing biblical passages that admonish the people of God to care for those who are among us in what is to them a strange and distant land. The reason is that caring for aliens is one of the most important concerns in the Bible. Perhaps the most intriguing example of how important this concern was to people in biblical times can be found in the story of Sodom and Gomorrah. Most of us know about the sexual sins of

Sodom and Gomorrah. As a matter of fact, we have given the name "sodomy" to same-gender sexual acts we deem to be repugnant. Most of us believe it was the sexual sins of these cities, as recorded in Genesis 19, that brought down the wrath of God and resulted in their destruction. But what most of us do not realize is that of equal seriousness in the eyes of God was the failure of those two wicked cities to show care and respect to the aliens who lived among them. Sodom and Gomorrah's indifference to the needs and sufferings of the strangers within their gates was such an abomination to God that it was as much the justification for raining down fire on these cities as was their deviant sexual behavior. Biblical passages such as Ezekiel 16:49 easily verify that claim:

> Behold, this was the iniquity of thy sister Sodom,
> pride, fulness of bread, and abundance of idleness was
> in her and in her daughters, neither did she strengthen
> the hand of the poor and needy.

I have a suspicion that the reasons we tend to ignore such verses while emphasizing the passage that deals with Sodom and Gomorrah's sexual perversity has much to do with the fact that too many of us Christians are more ready to provide proof texts that justify condemning homosexuals than we are ready to recognize that we are equally condemned if we fail to serve the aliens who live in our towns.

When it comes to Proposition 187, I suppose what most depresses me has been the horrendous silence of the churches of California following its passage. I was hoping the churches would stand up and say to illegal aliens like José Lopez, "If you are hungry, we will feed you, regardless of the vote on Proposition 187. If you are thirsty, we will give you something to drink, regardless of how the courts rule. If you are naked, we will clothe you, in spite of what the state legislature decides to do with you. If you are sick and the general hospitals or public clinics won't care for you, come to us. And if you are a stranger, do not fear—we will take you in.

"We will do these things because our Lord expects this of us and because He has warned us in His Word [see Matt. 25:31–46] that on that final judgment day we will be judged by how well we lived up to that expectation. We will do those things because the Jesus we love has told us that when we do these things for the least of our brothers and sisters, we are doing these things for Him." Jesus tells us in Matthew 25 that if we are to love Him and serve Him then we must love and serve Him as He comes to us through the alien who comes to us in need.

I am not about to argue the pros and cons of Proposition 187 so far as our national interests are concerned, but I am ready to argue that the Bible calls Christians to lovingly meet the needs of aliens—regardless of who they are. And if I am asked what I will do if the government forbids us to show such loving concern, I will have to answer, "I must obey God rather than man" (see Acts 5:29).

6

Does God Have a
Feminine Side?

MAINLINE DENOMINATIONS are still reeling from the fallout from the infamous "Re-Imagining Conference" held in Minneapolis, Minnesota, in November 1993. This conference, which was supported and financed by denominations that belong to the National Council of Churches, set off an uproar in the rank-and-file memberships of these mainline churches. Constituencies have demanded the firing of denominational officials who supported and funded it. The controversy over the conference is responsible for dividing local church congregations. There have been resolutions at the national meetings of mainline denominations that denounce and repudiate what went on at that notorious gathering.

When the conference was first called, most of us assumed its purpose was simply to permit Christian women to explore ways in which the church could become more relevant to the concerns of women. We also assumed that the participants would be looking for new ways to talk about the gospel that would free them from sexist values and prejudices. What happened turned out to be much more radical.

First of all, there was a lot of talk about Sophia. Passages from the Old Testament were cited as giving evidence of a deity other than the traditional Judeo-Christian God, Yahweh. Claims were made that Sophia, a female deity, had been known to the ancients and that they had deliberately suppressed mention of her in the Scriptures.

It was claimed that men, in an effort to maintain the subjugation of women, had deliberately edited out of the revelatory message of our faith all mention of this goddess. Without a female deity, women would have no choice but to worship the male God that was left. Doing this, it was claimed by the radical feminists at the conference, became one more instrument to oppress women. A religion that offered only a male God would lead to women worshiping masculinity and regarding their own femininity as something inferior, even something to be despised.

Such claims were not asserted without support. Evidence from archaeological finds and from the history of Mesopotamia, the cradle of civilization, were marshaled to support the case. To those who criticized the conference, radical feminists seemed to be rejecting the monotheism of Judaism and Christianity and calling for a belief in dual deities—Yahweh *and* Sophia.

This was bound to stir up a fuss when word of what happened at the conference got out to the mainstream membership of the sponsoring churches. The idea that money they had contributed to support their respective denominational programs should be used to encourage what many were calling "idolatry" initiated an uproar. What people had heard about the goings-on at the Re-Imagining Conference seemed to suggest that the "jealous God" of tradition had to make room for another deity that was equally demanding of worship. This was incredibly difficult to accept for those who had had a lifelong commitment to the Mosaic command:

> Thou shalt not make unto thee any graven image,
> or any likeness of any thing that is in heaven above, or
> that is in the earth beneath, or that is in the water under
> the earth:

Thou shalt not bow down thyself to them, nor serve
them: for I the LORD thy God am a jealous God, visiting
the iniquity of the fathers upon the children unto the
third and fourth generation of them that hate me.
(Exod. 20:4–5)

Talk about Sophia was not the only hot issue raised by the Re-
Imagining Conference. There were reports of things being said
at the conference that could only be construed as blasphemous.
Some women who had been especially hurt and oppressed by
men made angry claims that they had no need of "a male Savior"
and talked about Jesus in ways that denigrated His character. To
moderates and conservatives in mainline denominations, things
seemed to have gotten out of hand at the conference, and Christian feminism seemed to have moved outside of what really could
be called Christianity.

While I, myself have some very serious concerns about the Re-
Imagining Conference and am critical of some of the things that
were said and done there, I nevertheless believe there were some
good things that came out of it. First of all, I think it got concerned Christians in mainline churches to give serious attention
to what was happening in their denominations. The laity stood
up and began to take back their denominations from the somewhat elitist theologians who had previously set the tone and
established the programs being prescribed for local churches.
Whenever the laity is awakened like this, it gives hope for new
vitality in denominational life.

Second, theology was again made a serious matter to be dis-
cussed and defined at denominational gatherings. Most mainline
denominations have such diverse constituencies that there is a
reluctance to bring up theological concerns when representatives of various local churches get together. Theological debate
can make for division in the ranks, and those whose task it is to
keep denominational programs smoothly running and adequately financed are fearful of the consequences of all of this.
Unity is so important that most meetings that bring together

representatives from local churches are skillfully engineered to keep potentially divisive theological issues from ever getting to the floor for discussion. Yet without a clarifying theology to give purpose and direction, Christianity can be nothing more than a dead organization. Christianity comes alive when its people have a theological imperative to reach out to the world, to evangelize, and to lovingly work for the transformation of society. If the Re-Imagining Conference did nothing else except stir members of mainline churches to do some serious theological thinking, it may have made an incredibly important contribution to modern-day Christianity. For out of such reflection—and the evangelistic imperatives it can generate—can come revival.

But there may be one more vitally important consequence of the Re-Imagining Conference that, for our discussion here, might make it a blessing in disguise. It forced the rest of us in the church, especially complacent men, to do some serious thinking about women's issues. While most of us are by no means ready to abandon the God of the Bible, the upset caused by the Re-Imagining Conference has raised the question as to whether we men may have provided less than a valid interpretation of the God of the Bible. Even conservative Christians have been led to ask, "Has a male-dominated church read *into* the Scriptures an understanding of God that really is not there? Have we let men so bias our interpretation of the Scriptures that we have ended up with a distorted idea of what God is like and a very limited understanding of what the writers of the Bible were trying to tell us?"

I believe the Bible is infallible, but I do not believe those of us who read the Bible have an infallible understanding of what it says. As a consequence of the Re-Imagining Conference, we heard from some women who asked us to reconsider what we think the Bible is telling us about God and to ask if we've got it right. If we have to radically recast our thinking about God, it would not be the first time the church has done that. After all, isn't that what the Protestant Reformation was all about?

It may be that we men, for perhaps the first time in centuries, are being called to listen to what women find in the Scriptures. We are being asked to learn from them in order that whole new vistas of truth can open up for us all.

Let me share with you some of my thinking about all of this and some of the ways in which re-reading the Bible with an awareness of these concerns has led me.

I believe both men and women were created to be in the image of God. That is what I get from a simple reading of Genesis 1: "So God created man in his own image, in the image of God created he him; male and female created he them" (Gen. 1:27).

I believe that to be fully human is to so reflect God that when people look at us they ought to be able to get some glimpse about what God is like. But that doesn't happen. Something has gone wrong with us. The Bible calls it *the Fall*. Because of this fall, the wholeness of our humanity has been distorted. While there is something of the sacred left in us, we fail to express the "fullness" of what God intended.

This kind of thinking is not far removed from what psychologists who would not necessarily be considered Christians have to say about us. As an important case in point, let me in an overly simple way try to explain what Carl Jung, the one-time disciple of Freud, had to say about us.

It was Jung's belief that our society has taken some traits of the complete person and assigned them to females and others of these traits and assigned them to males. If males showed any of the traits of personhood that had been assigned to women, they were condemned. And similar condemnation was directed at women who expressed traits assigned to men. Each sex, consequently, was denied part of what it means to be a whole person, and that is part of the sickness that goes with the human condition. To be male in our Western culture often connotes assertiveness: hanging tough on principles, demanding strict obedience to rules and regulations, transcending any sentimentality and living in logic. And to be female has carried with it an expectation of submission, being governed by sympathy, being ready to put feelings above principles, and living by intuition.

I suppose what is worse is that we sometimes take our distorted view of what it means to be male and project it back on to God. There are times when we are prone to define God as the embodiment of patriarchal authoritarianism. I have heard sermons in which He comes across as some kind of transcendental Shylock demanding His pound of flesh. Too often our images of God lack the kind of mercy that our culture has characterized in feminine terms. Thus, we not only have an incomplete understanding of what it means to be male and female, we also end up with one-sided views about the nature of God.

There is a side of God that society chooses to call feminine. I always knew this. Even before the feminist movement demanded that I use inclusive language to publicly declare this truth, I saw this side of God in the Jesus who approached the world with what we would call a feminine sensitivity and appreciation. The way our Lord considered the lilies of the field and the way He gave pause to the smallest bird that might fall dead from a tree made me see this side of God most clearly.

If the side of God's character that society calls masculine was expressed by Jesus' strong declarations of truth and pronouncements on morality, what the world considers the female side of God was clear in His gentle sense of wonder while enjoying what the less perceptive would call the simple things of life. If I could have been around in Jesus' time, I do not think I would have so much wanted to see Him perform miracles and defy the self-righteous religionists as I would have enjoyed sneaking along after Him as He took His private walks. I would have loved peeking at Him from behind some boulder on a hillside near the Sea of Galilee and watching Him be charmed by all the sights and sounds that surrounded Him. I would have liked watching the way Jesus looked at all the people He met and seeing how He delighted Himself with simple food and the taste of water.

It is this side of Jesus that we have learned to call feminine that draws love out of me. Those traits that society conditions me to call feminine are the ones that make me want to sing duets with Him. When I think about these traits in Jesus that we are prone to regard as feminine, I want to throw out my arms to Him and be loved. I want to feel His sweetness and His gentleness. I want to sense Him touching me with His love.

When I was younger and tougher and trying to be a dead-serious prophet (and what young preacher doesn't have some desire to play such a role?) I was offended by a hymn that was loved by many of the elderly members of the congregation at the church I pastored. During the hymn-singing in our Sunday evening services there was a time for requesting favorites, and I could count on one of them to ask for "I Come to the Garden Alone." But the more I, myself, become an old guy, the more I understand why they requested that hymn. In my younger days, it seemed to reek of mushy sentimentality, and I always felt there was some neo-Freudian lovemaking going on between those who requested the hymn and Jesus.

Maybe I was right, but in my narrow and perverted thinking, I failed to see how pure and beautiful that could be. As I give up my Messianic tendencies and more and more simply surrender to the Messiah in love, this hymn becomes increasingly meaning-ful to me:

> *I come to the garden alone,*
> *While the dew is still on the roses;*
> *And the voice I hear, falling on my ear;*
> *The Son of God discloses.*
>
> *He speaks, and the sound of His voice*
> *Is so sweet the birds hush their singing.*
> *And the melody that He gave to me,*
> *Within my heart is ringing.*
>
> *I'd stay in the garden with Him*
> *Though the night around me be falling,*

But He bids me go; through the voice of woe,
His voice to me is calling.

And He walks with me, and He talks with me,
And He tells me I am His own;
And the joy we share as we tarry there,
None other has ever known.

In my youth I wanted to be like Martin Luther King, but the older I get, the more my role model becomes Saint Francis of Assisi. Of course there was a lot of Saint Francis in Dr. King and a lot of Dr. King in Saint Francis. But now it is the loving of Jesus in the Spirit that is becoming more and more a preoccupation of my life.

Not only do I love what society calls feminine in Jesus, but the more I know Jesus, the more I realize that Jesus loves those repressed traits in me that we are prone to call feminine. In a day and age when so many women are trying to rediscover the side of their humanity that the world deems masculine, I find Jesus is helping me appreciate forgotten dimensions of my own personality.

I find myself wanting to be the bride of Christ. I want Him to find in me—or if need be, to *create* in me—a sweetness and a sensitivity for all things and all people. I want more and more for Him to find in me—or to create in me—a gentle heart and an awareness of the goodness that lies in people around me and especially in my enemies.

Once I wanted to be the enemy of the enemies of Jesus. But little by little I am realizing that Jesus refuses to declare any of us to be His enemies, even though there are those who would like to dignify themselves by assuming the title. And the more I become aware that our Lord does not view His enemies as His enemies, the more difficult it becomes for me to define them as *my* enemies.

I want to learn to love those people who stand on the other side of the struggles in which I am engaged. I pray that Jesus will bring out in me that blessed trait, which some disparage as feminine weakness, that will enable me to find the good in the racist, the homophobe, the fascist, and the militarist. The side of me that the world calls masculine would want them destroyed. But as Jesus draws out what the world calls feminine in me, He makes me want to see them rescued by having the goodness that is in them overcome the evil.

There is that feminine side of me that must be recovered and strengthened if I am to be like Christ. And it is in the recovering of that side of my humanity that I find myself more and more willing and less and less afraid to be called "a bride of Christ."

Society has brought me up to suppress the so-called feminine dimensions of my humanness. But when Jesus makes me whole, both sides of who I am meant to be will be fully realized. Then, and only then, will I be fully able to love Jesus and accept His love for me. Until I accept the feminine in my humanness, there will be a part of me that cannot receive the Lord's love. And until I feel the feminine in Jesus, there is part of Him with which I cannot identify. What I long for, in the end, is to know the way He can love Himself through me and I can love myself through Him. Only when I know Him and His wholeness and am myself made whole will this happen. And when it does happen, I will be fully alive in Him and He in me. It is not yet, but it will be. And this is the good news:

Beloved, now are we the sons of God, and it doth not yet appear what we shall be: but we know that, when he shall appear, we shall be like him; for we shall see him as he is. (1 John 3:2)

7

What about Prayer
in Public Schools?

TODAY'S YOUNG PEOPLE present us with an array of incredibly complex problems. Drug use seems omnipresent. It is difficult to find a teenager these days who has not at least experimented with some illegal substance. An increasing number of crimes are committed by teenagers, and more and more of them are major crimes. Felonies committed by young people have increased 10,000 percent in the last three decades.

Most of our young people are likely to be sexually promiscuous. Today, 68 percent of African-American children are born out of wedlock, and the white female population is quickly catching up.

As we try to take in all of these horrendous facts, we are faced with the awareness that the institution we naively believed was going to help kids solve their problems has itself become one of the biggest problems of all. At an earlier time, when optimism prevailed, we thought our schools could educate our kids out of the behavioral patterns that could destroy them and threaten the future of the nations.

Now we know better. In fact, many people see the public school system not so much as the cure for all of our societal sicknesses as it is itself one of those sicknesses. Not only are schools failing to adequately teach kids the basics of reading, writing, and arithmetic, but they have become subcultures that too often socialize young people into a lifestyle that defies the values of Christianity.

In light of what is happening in the public school systems of this country, it is not surprising to discover that more and more parents are pulling their children out of public schools and either home-schooling them or putting them in Christian schools.

It has been said that for every complex problem there is a simple, easy-to-understand answer *that is wrong*. Such an answer is especially wrong when it comes to dealing with the complexities of all that troubles contemporary school-aged young people. The simplistic answer is to pass a law that would return prayer to the public schools.

Politicians love to say that putting prayer back in our schools is the answer to the problems of today's youth because saying this wins them votes in the religious community. Besides that, it is a "can't lose" proposition. After all, who can be opposed to praying, especially if the prayer really isn't a prayer at all but just a minute of silence?

Recently I saw a candidate for the U.S. Senate speak before a religious audience and win all kinds of nods of agreement as he explained that the problems that plague our young people started when prayer and Bible reading were taken out of the schools. He established in his simplistic argument that up until then, there were very few problems in the schools of America.

He compared a list of the concerns of teachers from before the Supreme Court took religious exercises out of the public schools to the concerns of teachers since that decision. When Bible reading and prayer were part of the everyday experiences of schoolchildren, the kinds of things teachers complained about were that their students sometimes chewed gum in class, that they would not stand in line properly, that they were often sloppy and threw paper on the floor, and that they often talked in class when they should have been listening.

A recent survey of teachers showed that their problems included students using drugs, the spread of sexually communicated diseases among students, fear of students carrying guns, and fear of being physically assaulted or raped by students.

"The reason for the change," said the candidate, "was that Bible reading and prayer were taken out of the classrooms." He made it sound as simple as that.

Please don't get me wrong! I think it is a very good thing for children to pray and hear something from the Word of God every day. But to claim that such simple religious exercises will solve the problems of the youth culture is naive, to say the least. To suggest that the serious social problems that have invaded our high schools would not exist today had Bible reading and prayer not been removed from the schools is stretching things a bit.

During the last thirty years, new forms of music have impacted young people with strongly sexual messages and stimulation. Rap musicians have put out recordings that glorify violence toward the police and ridicule all forms of authority. The "pop" heroes of the media have flaunted lifestyles that make drug use seem glamorous. Over the last few decades, couples have divorced with such frequency that half of the children in America are now growing up in single-parent homes or in "blended" families. The motion picture industry sometimes seems almost incapable of turning out a film that does not show nude bodies in orgiastic action. But while all of these things have had a destructive influence on our young people, probably the most detrimental influence on our youth has been television.

While Bible reading and prayer in the public schools would have been a good countervailing force against all of this, few of us believe it would have been able to prevent what the media have done to our kids. Losing Bible reading and prayer in the public schools was hardly decisive in determining what happened to the young people of America over the past few decades. Furthermore, a law that requires students to start each day with sixty seconds of silent meditation may do some of them a lot of good, but it will not turn things around for our troubled teenagers.

As we consider how to bring religion back into the school systems of America, there are a number of concerns that should be raised. First of all, if we believe teachers should read to their students from the Scriptures each day, what does that mean in places where the dominant religion is not traditional protestantism or Catholicism? For instance, in Utah, where the dominant religion is traditional Mormonism, should Baptist and Presbyterian kids have to sit through a reading from *The Book of Mormon* each day? And what would happen in Hawaii, where the dominant religion is Buddhism? Should Christian kids have to listen daily to readings from *The Compassionate Buddha*?

A democracy, I believe, is not so much the rule of the majority as it is a society in which it is safe to be in the minority. In a country like the United States, democracy means the majority should never be able to violate the consciences of the minority. No attempts should be made in a society such as ours to put children in a position where they are made to feel like outsiders because a religious belief that is different from their own is imposed on them. That should hold true just as much in those places where agnostics are in the minority as it is in those places where Christian children are in the minority. That is why the suggestion of sixty seconds of silent meditation in place of any kind of prayer or Scripture reading that favors one religious group over others seems like a good idea. In the quietude of that minute, each child would have some space to focus on what would nurture his or her soul or mind. No child would have to endure even the hint of religious tyranny from the majority.

While the suggestion to designate a time of silence at the start of the school day will do some good, there are other things that would have an even greater positive impact on the spiritual lives of children. First of all, we ought to consider the "released-time" option. The churches, synagogues, and mosques in a given neighborhood could ask the school board to set aside some time each week for religious education.

A good idea would be to have the children released from school an hour early on a particular day and bused directly to their respective houses of worship. There they could be given special classes in the faith and practices of their own religious traditions. This would provide some solid training, and it would give the churches an excellent opportunity to reach out to marginal Christians and casual church attenders. Providing released time for religious education is not a favor a school board may decide to grant or refuse. Released time for religious education is a *right* guaranteed by court decisions, a right that the religious leaders of a community can legitimately claim, and the school board must make it available.

Needless to say, putting together a teaching staff to handle the many children who would come to a church for released-time classes would be a major undertaking. But if the people of the congregation are not willing to make the sacrifices in the time, effort, and money that would be necessary to set up such a program, they are failing in the mission God has given them to do. The people of such a congregation, so far as I am concerned, have no right to complain about what the schools do or do not do about religious exercises. They really ought not to expect the teachers of a secular educational system to do, under compulsion of a new law, what God through the Scriptures has commanded His people to do.

Secondly, we can train our own children to lead Bible reading and prayer so that these things are so naturally a part of who they are that *they* will be able to share the Bible and pray with and for their classmates. While the courts *did* decree that neither the school board nor any employee of the school system has to be in any way involved in writing prayers, leading the students in prayer, reading Scriptures of any kind, or doing anything to initiate religious exercises, *students* are not forbidden from sharing the Scriptures or their faith with their classmates.

The logic of the courts is obvious. Since the teachers and administrators are paid by *all* the people and supposedly are the servants of *all* the people, they cannot do anything that would offend the values or beliefs of some or favor the values and beliefs of others. But none of this forbids those who are not acting as public servants from doing any of these things. This means there is nothing to prevent students from bearing witness to their classmates at recess and lunchtime or from using passages of Scripture as part of their own presentations to the class. Students cannot be denied their right to pray or read from the Bible because they are guaranteed that privilege by the first amendment of the Constitution. As currently interpreted by the courts, the first amendment, which guarantees the separation of church and state, forbids school officials and teachers from conducting religious exercises in school. But the first amendment also guarantees freedom of speech, allowing students the right to express what they believe and think.

Our responsibility—and this is very important—is to teach our children how to joyfully witness to a faith in Jesus that has great meaning to them, without acting in a "holier-than-thou" fashion that would turn off those who do not know our Lord. I meet adults who haven't learned the difference between letting others know that Christianity is a wonderful answer for their needs, and most unpleasantly forcing it on people. That's why I think it would be good for children to learn to joyfully share their faith at an early age.

Instead of complaining about what teachers and school officials cannot do to make God known in the schools, we should be training and encouraging the young people in our churches to take the initiative and make Bible reading and prayer part of what goes on at school every day.

If our Christian kids follow through on this suggestion and

take hold of this opportunity, we should expect that those of other religious persuasions will try to do the same. I believe that we should welcome this. It would be a good thing for kids to begin to know the various religions and beliefs that are held by their classmates. If young people are secure in their own beliefs, such exchanges of religious faith and practice will help them develop tolerance and understanding. Furthermore, I am convinced that if Christianity is clearly and faithfully set alongside other religions, it will shine forth as the truth that it is.

Still another option we should consider is the setting up of Christian club meetings before or after school hours. In some communities, the Fellowship of Christian Athletes, a ministry that has a special appeal to high-schoolers who love sports, has weekly meetings before the school day begins. In other communities, there are after-school meetings that bring students together for Bible study, prayer, discussion, and evangelism. Such meetings are allowed. According to the Religious Restoration Act passed into law in November 1993, they can even be held within school buildings.

Sometimes school officials, unaware that they are acting illegally, will try to bar such meetings on the school premises. If that happens, they need to be challenged. If you need help or guidance in pursuing such a challenge, you might contact:

THE CHRISTIAN LEGAL SOCIETY
4208 Evergreen Lane, Suite 222
Annandale, Virginia 22003
(703) 642 - 1070

School officials sometimes are afraid that by letting Christian groups meet in the school, they will receive criticism from some quarters. Consequently, they say no to requests for the use of school space for Christian meetings. They have to be informed that any such refusal is a violation of the constitutional rights of those making the request. Other groups from Communists to

Satan worshipers have been able to get the use of school buildings for their meetings. It is unconscionable that school officials could then turn around and deny a group of Christian students the opportunity to hold *their* meetings on school premises.

Unfortunately, one of the main reasons Christians have been misled into thinking they do not have the kinds of rights I have been describing is that some Christians on radio and television have misled them. These broadcasters play on the fears of their listeners and try to scare them into thinking the government is controlled by evil people who are trying to take away the rights of believers. Their campaigns of misinformation are often designed to get listeners to send in contributions to finance their own so-called struggles to regain our freedom of religion. Beyond that, some of these broadcasters have political motives. They are able to use these same scare tactics to round up support for their favorite candidates by promising that those candidates will work to restore certain religious rights when in reality those rights were never taken away.

To take advantage of the existing opportunity to make the gospel message and the truths of the Bible better known in the public school system will require a great deal of creative thinking, planning, and hard work. No simple passing of a law guaranteeing sixty seconds of silent meditation at the start of the school day, as good an idea as that is, will make the kind of spiritual impact on kids that is needed. The alarmists are right when they tell us the youth of our nation are in serious trouble and are verging on self-destruction. But the solution is not as simple as passing a constitutional amendment to guarantee prayer in the public schools.

In the midst of all this talk about how to ensure that our kids start off each day with prayer and Bible reading, we may be ignoring the obvious. If parents *really* want to be sure *their* kids get the daily inspiration and direction they need, they must provide that inspiration and direction themselves. Only then will their children be equipped to share their faith with others at school.

If, instead of just complaining about what the school system fails to provide, Christian parents and their children got up a little earlier to read some Scripture and pray before anybody even left the house, something wonderful would begin to happen. Perhaps we then would see the beginnings of the changes in our kids we have all been longing for. It seems a bit hypocritical to require the school system to do for our kids something we are unwilling to do for them ourselves.

8

Should Christians
Quit Teaching in the
Public School System?

IT BOTHERS ME when I hear bombastic preachers taking out
after the public school system. I have heard it said that public
schools are nothing more than institutions that indoctrinate
children and young people with the beliefs and values of secular
humanism.

These preachers often urge parents to pull their children out
of public schools. Some preachers warn that kids will be led
astray by teachers who pollute their students' minds with anti-
Christian values ranging from alternative sexual lifestyles to New
Age religion.

Sadly, there is enough evidence that such things actually happen in public schools to give some support to these alarmist
claims. There *are* abuses in public education that should be challenged. There *are* trends that ought to be checked. And there *are*
practices that have to be questioned. But after Christian critics
have voiced all of their complaints about what is wrong with public schools, there are still strong grounds for asserting that these
schools can be good places for Christians to be.

I am worried these days as I see more and more children
leaving public schools to attend private Christian schools. I

understand the rationale behind these moves, but I wonder what the future holds for public schools as massive numbers of Christian students leave them. I am concerned about what the public school system will be like if increasing numbers of Christian parents disengage from the Parent-Teacher Associations and school boards of public schools.

Most of all, I am concerned about the long-term effects if Christian teachers are no longer a presence in the public school system.

Have we so denigrated public schools through our religious rhetoric that Christian collegians are no longer considering public school teaching as a profession? Are we making those who teach in the public school system feel as though they are wasting their lives and ought instead to teach in Christian schools?

I have had teachers tell me that the public school system is so scorned in their churches that they are embarrassed to let anyone know what they do for a living. Furthermore, teachers themselves say they are frustrated in the public school system and feel as though their hands are tied so far as exercising a Christian witness is concerned.

But after all the negatives about public school teaching have been given, we do not have the whole story. All across America, there are still hundreds of thousands of Christians who find in public school teaching an opportunity to serve Jesus and reach children and teenagers with the love of Christ.

Not long ago, I was asked to lead an evangelistic crusade in a town in Kentucky. The meetings were held at the high school football field, with the people sitting in the bleachers. Each evening, a couple of thousand people showed up. This seemed pretty good to me, since this county-seat community had a population of only about ten thousand.

The second night, I noticed a young man leading a group of about twenty-five high school students into the meeting. They all sat together in the stands and seemed to be having a wonderful time together. It was obvious to me that this young man had great rapport with the students, and the whole group entered enthusiastically into the program of the evening. I assumed the young man was a youth leader from one of the local churches and that the young people with him were part of his youth group. It was not until later that I learned he was a teacher at the local high school and the young people with him were some of his students.

At the end of my evangelistic sermon, I gave an invitation for people to come forward if they wanted to surrender their lives to Christ. Several of the young people who had come to the meeting with the young schoolteacher did so. At least a dozen of them came forward to commit themselves to live under the lordship of Christ.

I had a chance to talk to that teacher after the meeting, and I asked him how he got around the requirements that are laid upon public school teachers to keep religion out of the classroom. I figured he was going to tell me that in this largely Protestant community he was able to get away with things that would not be possible for teachers in large cities like Louisville. "How did you pull off getting your students to this meeting?" I inquired.

"I invited them," was his simple answer.

"Yes," I responded, "but how are you able, in a public school high school, to invite your students to a church meeting?"

"I don't," was his reply. "I would never even think of trying to reach out to them during school hours or on the school grounds. I do my inviting during after-school hours, especially in the evenings. Some of them I call on the telephone, and I do a lot of my inviting when I bump into these kids at McDonald's or see them at the movies."

I have thought a lot about that wonderful Christian teacher since that night. What he had done would not be possible in every town or every school situation. It would not even be the *right* thing to do in some places. It would be unwise and unkind to do what this young teacher had done if some of his students had been put in the uncomfortable position of having either to go somewhere their parents did not want them to be or feel left out of that part of the class that was "in" with the teacher. But in this Protestant community, *all* of his students had come along with him. The families who were not actively Protestant were probably not actively anything else either, and no one minded their kids enjoying the evening out.

As I talked to that young teacher, surrounded by boys and girls who obviously loved and admired him, I knew without a doubt that he and the Holy Spirit would have worked out a witness that was kind and fair and winsome in whatever place he had found himself teaching.

It was once said by Saint Francis that we should preach the gospel all day long—and sometimes we should even use words.

This teacher undoubtedly did just what Saint Francis was talking about. All day long he showed love for his students and gave them Jesus without uttering a word about Christianity. Then after school was over, he was able to draw on this spiritual capital he had built up in their lives as he made appeals to them for the cause of Christ.

Are most Christian public school teachers failing to seize their opportunity to witness to their students and share Christ with them simply because the law says they cannot do it during school hours? Are teachers losing an incredible opportunity to follow up on the nonverbal witness for Christ that they can express in their everyday walk before their students? Might not teachers reach their students with the gospel simply by taking advantage of loving relationships they have built one day at a time?

I know teachers work hard all day and when that closing bell rings, they want to take it easy. I know that during their after-hours time teachers have to prepare lesson plans and mark papers. I realize that teaching is a time-demanding job. But if Christian teachers care enough, they will go far beyond the call of duty to reach their students with the transforming love and message of Christ.

Wouldn't it be wonderful if Christian teachers made commitments to visit their students, get to know their parents, and become personally involved in their lives? The possibilities for touching the lives of students for Christ seems limitless. It may be that public school teaching is one of the best launching platforms for those who want to introduce the youth of this generation to the gospel.

The need for Christians to be in the public school system is particularly great in the troubled cities of this country. In some of the "battle zones" of urban America, schools are dangerous and difficult places, and only those with a real sense of calling will want to teach there. It is the task of the church to challenge teachers to recognize that those urban schools are mission fields, places where Christians ought to be doing ministry.

Urban Promise, the missionary organization I helped start in Camden, New Jersey, involves hundreds of college-aged young people in a variety of programs for inner-city youth. These collegians do after-school tutoring, lead Bible studies, sponsor cultural-enrichment programs, and reach out to inner-city kids through a variety of other activities. They do their best to reach the children and teenagers of Camden with the gospel of love and hope — something that is desperately needed in Camden, where over 90 percent of the newborns last year were born out of wedlock, and where drugs and crime are destroying most teenagers. According to the January 20, 1992, issue of *Time* magazine, fewer than one-third of those who enter Camden high schools ever graduate. And many of those who do graduate have difficulty getting jobs because they graduate as functional illiterates.

Given all of the horrendous circumstances of Camden, it is not surprising how many of the young missionaries who serve with Urban Promise choose to go into public school teaching. Many of the city kids they work with day in and day out come from homes of neglect and abuse, and one of the best opportunities to make a difference in their lives is through the schools.

There is no point in even talking about Christian schools for the majority of those youngsters because their families are not willing, or even able, to make the kinds of sacrifices required to send them to Christian schools. But these children do get enrolled in the public school system of the city. Whether they attend regularly and whether their school experiences help or hurt them has everything to do with who they meet there. Getting to know a teacher who cares can make all the difference in the world for inner-city kids.

The collegians who spend a summer working with Urban Promise become aware of that, and that is why so many of them choose to become teachers in urban public schools. They won't be the kinds of teachers who simply mark students absent when they do not show up but instead will follow up with phone calls or visits to find out what is going on in their students' lives. They will be the kinds of teachers who are available after class to counsel kids through some of their painful problems and transitions. They want to be role models for inner-city kids who so desperately need some positive role models to emulate.

This special kind of missionary to urban youth was recently modeled by a young man I will call Leonard Johnson. I first met Leonard when he came from his small Christian college in the Midwest to work with kids on the streets of Camden in our summer program. He had come just for one summer, but he got hooked. Once Leonard experienced the spontaneity of city kids, tasted their hunger for affection, and sensed their special need for attention, he could not leave.

Leonard now teaches eighth grade in a school located in one of the worst slums in Philadelphia, just across the river from Camden. He has chosen to live in the same community where he teaches, has joined a church in the neighborhood, and is involved in a variety of civic organizations. In many ways, Leonard has become a leader in the community. His story, just one of many I could tell, will give you some idea of the many kinds of good things being done quietly and without fanfare by Christian teachers who have become sensitized to deprived children.

I stopped by his apartment one evening to attend a planning meeting for an upcoming Christian youth rally. While we were talking, the phone rang. It was one of Leonard's students, who called him because she didn't know who else to call. She was beside herself with fear and confusion because the police had just arrested her mother for prostitution and she had been left alone to care for her two younger brothers.

Leonard called the pastor of his church and asked him to meet us at the girl's home, located in a government housing project down the street. With me tagging along, he rushed over to his student's house to see what he could do to help.

When we got there, we found her two brothers crying hysterically as they asked over and over if the police were going to beat up their mother. The student greeted us with the downcast eyes of sorrowful despair I have seen too often in children who have no childhood. She did not say much. She didn't have to. What needed to be done was clear.

When the pastor came, he immediately made a call to arrange for someone to come and care for the children. They needed some meals. The house was a mess and needed to be cleaned.

Leonard called a lawyer friend who lived nearby and asked him to handle getting the mother out of jail. It seemed like no time at all before he had things under control. What a joy it was to watch the reactions of that eighth-grade girl as she gained a sense of knowing she was being cared for by somebody who loved her.

An hour later, a friendly older woman from the church arrived and took charge. She told us to go on home and said she would get the children to bed and take care of things until the mother got home. But before we left, Leonard called us all to bow our heads in prayer. And when we lifted our eyes, I saw peace in the smile on that schoolgirl's face. "This," I said to myself, "is ministry at its best."

When it comes to inner-city schools, it is essential that we have teachers who see them as mission fields. It is also essential that the rest of us view urban schools as mission fields. Specifically, we must find ways to support these teachers who willingly choose to take on the difficult task of teaching in these places.

In Philadelphia, John White Sr., a deacon in my church, has come up with a brilliant plan to get church people involved with the young people in the city schools. If it were carried out effectively, his plan could be a godsend to the teachers of these schools, who all too often feel alone in their struggles to do a very difficult job. John's plan is to get specific churches to "adopt" specific schools and to commit themselves to helping improve those schools. An important part of that task is building up the Parent-Teacher Associations. Few things have proven to provide more encouragement to teachers or to raise the level of learning than getting parents involved in the education process.

John is proposing that church people work along with school authorities to build up attendance at the PTA meetings. It would be the task of the church people to call parents on the phone and personally urge them to attend PTA meetings each month. They would offer transportation to those who need it. Follow-up calls and personal visits to these parents are all part of John's plan. The sad fact is that less than 1 percent of parents of children in the public school system attend PTA meetings, and in many schools, the teachers and administrators have given up even trying to hold such meetings. John hopes to change all of that. He believes that within a year it would be possible to get as many as half of these parents involved with their children's teachers and supportive of what those teachers are trying to do.

Studies indicate that when boys and girls get special attention their learning shows marked improvement. After-school tutoring programs such as the ones run by the young Urban Promise missionaries make a tremendous impact on school kids. But as significant as the academic improvements that come from such efforts are, they do not even begin to match the impact that comes when parents pay significant attention to their children's learning. When *parents* become partners with schoolteachers, when they verify that homework gets done, when they sit with their children and provide encouragement and help, when they constantly check with teachers to make sure their children are not cutting school or lying about having no homework, then the city's schools will begin once again to be places where the hopes and dreams of millions of city kids can be realized.

Suburban churches, too, can get involved as partners with inner-city schools to carry out John White's plan. And when the teachers of those city schools experience this groundswell of support, they will respond with new enthusiasm and commitment to their difficult task. While it may take a lot of time and energy on the part of church people, what is being suggested here is simple enough to implement. And it seems to me that results are just about guaranteed.

Why not get your church involved in such an arrangement? Why not challenge an adult Sunday school class or the men's fellowship to take on such a challenge? Why not step out and give support not only to Christians who teach in the public schools but to all teachers who are striving to rescue kids from overwhelmingly difficult circumstances.

John White's plan is to rebuild the commitment of parents to the teachers who teach their children. He is planning to make it happen, but this task requires the help of church people on a massive scale. It's a "cop-out" for us simply to say, "These schools are hopeless," throw up our hands, and walk away from the plight of urban campuses.

We need to encourage Christians to teach in public schools, be they urban, suburban, or rural; we must constantly affirm these teachers in their efforts. I know of one church that has an annual appreciation dinner for the teachers of that community.

And with this important gesture, they send this message to everyone in town: "We love and support our public school teachers."

It is hard to know what future trends for education in this country will be, but the Lord who has called us to go into *all* the world to preach the gospel certainly expects us to go into the public schools of this country bearing, in Jesus' name, our witness of love and concern.

9

Is Television Demonic?

COMPETING with television has been a problem for the church ever since "the tube" became a part of our lives. The amount of time we give to watching television staggers the imagination. One rather conservative estimate is that the typical American watches television five hours a day.

It is pretty obvious that having been seduced by television makes it difficult for us to give our lives to Jesus. When it comes to time, we are more committed to television than we are to service to His kingdom. Years ago, churches started dropping Sunday evening services because they were no match for Ed Sullivan, and youth leaders had a hard time getting kids away from their TV sets to attend youth fellowship meetings.

Beyond competing with TV for time, the church has to deal with the emotional commitments people make to television. TV gets such a strong hold on some people that the TV characters sometimes become more real and more important than their own family members.

A minister friend of mine told me a story that would have been funny had it not been so tragic. He told me about a Wednesday night prayer meeting at his church in which a woman asked for prayer for one of the characters in the soap opera she regularly watched. My friend told her, "But the people in your soap opera aren't real!"

"I know," she answered, "but the young woman I'm telling you about *is* going through a difficult time and needs our prayers."

On Super Bowl Sunday, the loss of the game by the home team can put fans into incredible fits of depression. And in homes ranging from derelict dwellings in city slums to palatial mansions in wealthy suburbs, there are young mothers who pay more attention to television than to their own children. There is little doubt that for too many people television has become a preoccupation with which the church finds it difficult to compete.

Another concern about television is the values it communicates. There are those who argue that television does not so much create values as it reflects them. We've all heard the line that the media only provide a mirror image of what is going on in our everyday lives. Well, I do not believe that!

Recently, the most authoritative study of sexual behavior in America gave statistical evidence that last year only 4 percent of married people committed adultery. You would never know that from television. What comes across in show after show is that everybody is doing it. When Dan Quayle attacked the *Murphy Brown* show because it made having a baby out of wedlock seem both commonplace and acceptable, he was greeted by a storm of scornful criticism. But Quayle was right on target, contended the *Atlantic Monthly* in a major article, and the *Atlantic Monthly* is hardly a publication noted for its conservative leanings. President Clinton, the leader of the opposition party, lent support to Quayle's opinion, saying, "I was making Quayle's speech before Quayle did."

The media don't reflect reality; they create it. This is true not only about sex. It is also true about crime. Statistics show conclusively that there is a decline in crime in the major cities of America, but you would never get this impression from talking to the American people, who get their information from television. Most Americans, statistics to the contrary, believe crime is on the increase, and they are increasingly afraid of venturing out of their homes. Things are by no means good in America, but they are not nearly as bad as prime-time television makes them out to be.

For the church, the value orientation of television poses special problems. It is difficult to promote the kind of sexual purity that has been traditionally preached from the pulpit in the face of this overpowering medium. Television makes the values that prohibit premarital intercourse and demand a lifelong commitment between husbands and wives seem quaint and outdated. Modesty seems to have been totally discarded by those of us who have become used to viewing what an earlier generation would have found lewd. How do we tell young people that sexual abstinence is expected of them when they are daily bombarded by MTV videos that urge them to seek instant sexual gratification? How do we convince them they should wait until marriage for sex when visual images and drumbeats constantly get their hormones flowing hot?

Less noticeable, but just as devastating to Christian values, is the affluent lifestyle that television leads its viewers to believe is their entitlement. Everyone, suggest the ads, deserves "a break today," and that break means the right to buy what the ads are selling.

Consider how the popular media are now overcoming differences that once existed between the satisfactions provided by spiritual well-being and the satisfactions that come from consumer goods. For instance, Coca-Cola (in what may be the most famous television ad of all time) replicated the biblical imagery of the day of Pentecost. In the ad, people from various ethnic groups from around the world assembled on a hilltop, holding hands and singing: "I want to teach the world to sing in perfect harmony . . . "

But the force that created this perfect harmony for broken

humanity, conquered the curse of Babel, unified us, and overcame our sense of separateness was not the Holy Spirit, according to the ad. It was Coca-Cola! For America, Coke has become "the real thing."

Think about the way the intimacy of biblical *koinonia* (fellowship) is portrayed as being created simply by buying the right kind of beer. In another famous ad, we are invited to be the unseen guests of some sportsmen having a cookout on the back porch of a rustic lodge. They have just finished a good day of fishing and are cooking some of their catch. As they pull the tops off their beer cans, one of them comments, "It just doesn't get any better than this." Then, as the camera pulls back to give us a good overall view of the idyllic scene, a deep baritone voice sings out, "Here's to good friends; tonight is kind of special . . ."

Through this ad, the viewers are told that this brand of beer will deliver far more than what is in the can. We are being told that the right beer can overcome the loneliness of the soul.

In TV ads, it is as though the ecstasy of the spirit experienced by a Saint Theresa or a Saint Francis can be reduced to the gratification coming from a particular car, and the kind of love Christ compared to His love for His church can be expressed by buying the right wrist watch "for that special person in your life." In all this media hype, things are sold to us on the basis that our deepest emotional and psychological needs will be met by having the right consumer goods.

In earlier times, spiritual gratification was presumed to come only via spiritual means. Thus, people could be urged to choose between the things of this world and the blessings of God. Now, that duality has been overcome. Ours is an age in which spiritual blessings are being promised to those who buy material things. The spiritual is being absorbed by the physical. The fruit of the spirit, suggest the media, can be had without God and without spiritual disciplines. It is not simply that we are materialists who crave the goods that flood our markets but that we are now a people who have been made to believe subconsciously that we will find in these things an end to the spiritual longings at the center of our being.

Television also has had a major impact on the sexual mores and folkways of America. Messages about sexuality, often involving sadomasochism and the denigration of woman, are common fare on TV—especially on MTV. The MTV cable network brings to teenagers videos that depict orgiastic promiscuity and sexual bondage as normal modes of behavior. The impact of all of this has been overpowering and is not likely to be overcome by an occasional Sunday school lesson on a healthy and biblically prescribed sexuality. When a vice president of MTV was asked what influence his station had on teenagers, he answered, "We don't influence teenagers—we own them."

I do not debate his contention; I only ask what it means when teenagers who are hooked on MTV say, "Jesus Christ is Lord!" Does Jesus own them or does MTV?

What is particularly depressing is the way in which television socializes preschool children. Their language, attitudes, and outlook on life are all molded primarily through television and only to a much lesser extent by their parents. Children have lost their imagination for play and want only to sit transfixed by the likes of Big Bird.

My son is trying to raise his children without having television be a major part of their lives, but it's hard. Their playmates and schoolmates constantly talk about what they watch on television. One day while visiting at our house, my three-year-old granddaughter piously told me, "We don't watch TV at our house because my daddy says that talking to people is more fun." Then she paused and added sadly, "But it isn't true."

What my granddaughter knew all too well is that television is easily the most entertaining thing going. Next to it, the whole world seems boring and dull. And to a generation reared on television, something has to be pretty amazing to get their attention away from the tube. The net effect on society is that nothing will be given much time or energy unless it is reduced to fun and entertainment. That goes for the news, for education, and it certainly goes for Christianity. If people are going to listen to anything, it must first be reduced to punchy and entertaining sound bites. Everything else is rejected.

Those professionals who put on the evening news know this. Earthquakes in Japan or hurricanes in Florida must all be reduced to entertaining video footage with a zippy (and probably gorgeous) newsperson providing thirty seconds of smiling commentary. Tragedy is turned into entertainment, and after a few short flashes of suffering the viewer hears a voice say, "And now this word from our sponsor."

But even the ads are not a time to turn away from the sets to pay attention to something else. Sponsors have worked hard to make the ads even more entertaining than the shows. They have done their best to ensure that nobody leaves the room to go for a sandwich or a beer.

The secret of the ads is "technical changes." The best ads throw so many images at us in such rapid succession that we find ourselves mesmerized by what they say. A good Pepsi ad throws out pictures of beautiful young people in a succession of fun activities ranging from surfing and dancing to hugging and kissing. None of the images lasts long enough to allow even a trace of boredom to set in. I know of one ad that put on the TV screen sixty different images in just twenty seconds. A Sunday morning sermon is highly unlikely to seem fast-moving by comparison.

For the most part, church leaders have gone on about their business as though nothing has changed. Sunday morning worship services are pretty much what they were a hundred years ago. A glance at the average church bulletin clearly demonstrates that what unfolds between eleven and twelve on Sunday mornings differs very little from the usual order of worship prescribed in a New England church at the turn of the century. For most churches, it is as though the electronic media never happened. There is, in most churches, such an indifference to how TV has changed the mind-set of the congregation that a social scientist would have to call it an extreme case of denial of reality.

The results, for those churches that have refused to face the fact that television has socialized their members into a new state of consciousness, have been all too obvious. They have experienced an erosion of attendance at Sunday morning worship and are faced with the fact that those who do attend do so, for the most part, out of a sense of obligation. Few church attenders arise on Sunday mornings to sing with the psalmist, "I was glad when they said unto me, let us go into the house of the LORD" (Ps. 122:1).

Perhaps church never was very exciting, but at least what happened on Sunday morning did not come across as quite so humdrum as it does nowadays. In bygone days, stoic and prosaic worship services did not have to compete with the fast-moving excitement of television shows. The theological discourse called "the sermon" did not have to stand in contrast to the sensationalism of TV dramas that use up millions of dollars to ensure that they hold people's interest.

People reared on television do not reject God or Christianity; they are just lured away from them. They do not make a conscious decision to give up on the church; they simply and gradually bid it a fond farewell.

Young people are not antireligious. To the contrary, they are fascinated by the mystical side of life. When asked why they don't want to go to church, young people generally answer with one short sentence: "Church is boring!" They still like spiritual things. Just note their attraction to the New Age movement. But they pay little attention to any form of religion that does not conform to the cannons of entertainment prescribed by the electronic media. The fascination of the New Age movement is that it is endorsed by TV stars and has its own increasingly popular genre of music. New Age stuff is a feeling without intellectual content. It is an instantaneous experience that requires no arduous sacrifice and demands no restraint of passion.

It has perfect "functional fit," as sociologists would say, with the lifestyle of a generation that sees reality through the eyes and ears of television.

Those churches that ignore all of this and go about their religious business as usual go through a gradual but very observable decline. Pulpit committees that remember "the good old days" when their churches were filled go looking for superstar preachers who will deliver spellbinding sermons that will "pack them in." These churches do not realize they are struggling against "principalities, against powers, against the rulers of the darkness of this world" (Eph. 6:12). What makes matters worse is that young preachers are usually led to believe if they were just "good enough" they could meet such expectations. No wonder so many of them burn out and give up with a sense of having failed. The expectations of people who live with television are almost always far beyond the ministers' ability to meet them. In light of all of this, is it too much to suggest that television is a demonic thing that is killing churches and oppressing God's servants?

To say that television is demonic may sound a little extreme until we begin to figure out what it has done to those in our society whom sociologists call "the truly disadvantaged." Leaders in the African-American community are alarmed over what TV is doing to their children. They point out that the typical African-American child is watching more than six and a half hours of television every day. They further claim that this extensive television watching is a primary reason why their children are not learning to read. The lure of TV has disengaged the children from books, causing many of our most socially disinherited African-American young people to grow up to be functional illiterates.

Adding to the problems faced by educators of children is the illusion that certain television programs like *Sesame Street* are contributing to the learning process. But such programs do not actively *engage* children. The boys and girls who watch these shows sit passively. There is no real interaction between what is happening on the television screen and the child who sits with his or her eyes glued to the set. Without real engagement and interaction, effective learning just does not happen.

The experts say that children learn from *doing*, not just from watching. *Sesame Street* is entertainment disguised as learning. When children *see* the alphabet letters sing and dance on television, they are not really learning how to *write* those letters; nor do they become actively involved in putting letters together to form words. Watching Big Bird do something is not the same kind of learning process children enjoy when they do it themselves.

All of this discussion by African-American educators leads to just one conclusion: Television has become a major factor in destroying the reading and learning skills of African-American children. There are a host of problems that flow from this failure to learn, such as dropping out of school without a basic education. These children too often find themselves unemployable when they grow up. Crime can easily become a vocation when the lack of an education curtails other options. Girls get pregnant because having children is sometimes seen as the only way they can establish themselves as "grown up."

The list of problems that African-American children face which can be related to watching television are legion. In a larger sense, they are problems that affect all children these days, because all children watch television. But the problem becomes especially severe for African-American children due to the fact that African-American children watch more TV than children in other ethnic communities. The social and economic problems that plague the African-American community make their children more prone to watching television. The cultural advantages that money can buy are not available to them; more than 46 percent of African Americans fall below the poverty line. Children in these circumstances are often devoid of the kinds of life experiences that would broaden their horizons and stimulate their thinking and learning. Passive sitting in front of the TV is no substitute for real life.

Jerry Meander, the author of *Four Arguments for the Elimination of Television*, points out that as ironic as it may seem, television actually contributes significantly to creating hyperactive kids. Some of the most uncontrollable boys and girls in urban classrooms are the product of television watching, he says.

Meander explains that when children sit for hours in front of a television set, energy builds up that is later worked out of their systems through hyperactivity. Children who sit too long become uncontrollable once they get up and get moving.

In light of what we know about the effects of television on the African-American community, it is no wonder that Cornel West, the head of the black studies program at Harvard University, argues that television has had a demonic effect on African-American children and teenagers. In addition to diminishing their learning and pushing them into the kind of hyperactivity that makes functioning in a classroom setting almost impossible, West points out that television has become a primary force in generating a sense of *nihilism* among black teenagers. Television, he says, has communicated to young people a lifestyle that allows them to believe that the seeking of pleasure and the acquiring of possessions is what life is all about. From the ads to the videos played on MTV, the message is the same: The meaning of life is the immediate gratification of desires. With such a way of life driven into the consciousness of its young people, it is no wonder that life has become dangerous and empty on the streets of the black community. And it is no wonder that African-American teenagers, more and more, evidence an absence of the kinds of meaningful long-range goals in life that would motivate them to achievement and generate hope.

West is well aware that what television is doing to African-American children and teenagers it is doing to all children and teenagers. He argues, however, that it is happening more among his people because his people watch more television and have fewer alternatives to the passive escape route that TV provides for them from their often-oppressive lives.

Satan could not come up with a better instrument than television for the destruction of children in general and of African-American children in particular. The TV set looks so benign sitting there in the living room. But it is an instrument for turning off the brain to real engagement with life and learning. It seduces young people into a nihilistic lifestyle that makes pleasure-seeking their *raison d'être*. And it is a propagator of a consumeristic lifestyle that drives children to see life as nothing more than the accumulation of things. It is no wonder that so many people say, "The one who dies with the most toys wins!"

Over and over in my thinking—and in this book—I refer back to the apostle Paul's declaration in Ephesians 6:12 reminding us that in struggling against evil we are not only up against the desires and weaknesses of our own flesh, but also have to fight against what he calls "principalities" and "powers." Paul made it clear that spiritual survival not only requires that we bring "the will" (our sexual desires, our hunger for praise, our jealousies, and all our other impulses and drives) into subjection to the will of God, but that we deal with those "powers" outside of ourselves that exercise control over what we think and do.

It is common to refer to those "powers," as Paul called them, as demons or evil spirits. Hendrick Berkhof, in his classical little book *Christ and the Powers*, supports the idea that such an interpretation is true for Paul's intentions. But Berkhof goes on to point out that when Paul wrote about principalities and powers, he was referring to all of those trans-human forces Satan uses to get hold of and to destroy God's people. Berkhof would have no trouble assigning television to this category of demonic instruments.

There is, of course, another side to television. Berkhof reminds us that it is God who has created the principalities and powers. And he goes on to stress that part of God's plan of salvation is to rescue these principalities and powers from their demonic use and make them into instruments of His will.

God, Berkhof would argue, wants to transform television from a destructive force in our culture into a means to bless people and make their lives more joyful. This can be done. But it can be done only when, with the aid of the Holy Spirit, we bring this principality and power under control. That, of course, is what the Bible calls us to do (see Eph. 1:19–23).

Prayerfully, we should consider the following:

1. How much television is too much? Certainly it is poor stewardship of our time to spend more than a couple of hours a day in front of a television set.

2. How do we decide what we should and should not watch? Do we decide at all, or do we simply flip the dial and "channel surf," looking for something to preoccupy our attention?

3. Is what we watch acceptable to God? We never watch alone. He is always with us, and what we watch He watches through our eyes.

4. Are we carefully discussing what is viewed with our children so we know what they are taking in from it all?

5. Are we becoming addicted to television? Is it possible to turn off the set and not watch anything for weeks at a time? Or is such a "cold turkey" exercise too much to handle? If the latter is the case, you need to go to God in prayer and ask Him to help you find deliverance.

There are good uses for television. I am convinced of that. But TV is so seductive and has such power to pull us into its grip that we must be aware of its demonic potentialities and be ever vigilant concerning its effects on us and our children. If television is getting out of control in your life or in the lives of your family members, maybe the best thing to do is to *kill it*!

10

Is That Preacher Who Killed the Abortion Doctor Guilty of Murder?

A MAN SHOOTS up an abortion clinic, killing a couple of the people who were in charge of arranging abortions. At another clinic, a doctor who performed abortions regularly is murdered.

While most of those in the pro-life movement react with shocked abhorrence, there are some who deem the men with the guns heroes. The result of their actions—a reduction of the number of abortionists in America—more than justifies the murders in the eyes of certain radically committed pro-life activists. "After all," they say, "just look at the statistics."

The statistics indeed are impressive. When abortion clinics come under violent attacks, the number of abortions drops. The number of doctors willing to perform abortions goes into rapid decline. Certain hospitals announce that because of threats of violence, they will no longer permit abortions to be performed. Abortion clinics close in such numbers that in many areas of the country there are none to be found.

If you are really into the pro-life movement, you have to quietly rejoice in these consequences and thank God for them, even though you probably feel some regret over the people who were killed.

There are moralists who will shriek their opposition and claim that these radicals are dangerous and that those who do not cry out against them are justifying murder. These moralists have a point, but so do the radical pro-lifers. If they believe abortion is murder, then isn't there some logic to murdering the murderers?

To make a comparison, let's consider whether there might have been a certain morality during World War II in the killing of a couple of Gestapo guards so that the lives of a few hundred innocent Jews could be saved.

Unless you are a pacifist pro-lifer, what problems do you have with killing the abortion doctors? Is it not justifiable to kill in the defense of the weak and helpless? Is it not right to kill a few of the guilty to save the many innocent? If the struggle is really a war, then why be upset that a few of the enemies get shot up in winning a necessary victory?

And yet, there still seems to be something wrong with this kind of talk. It generates an uneasiness even among the most ardent pro-life advocates. Pro-lifers are haunted by a strange uncertainty that keeps them from making the same kind of radical commitment made by those who would kill in the name of saving lives.

It is this uncertainty that leads most Christians to oppose the violence that seems more and more evident in the movement to stop abortions. While most evangelical Christians have emotional commitments that lead them to be strongly pro-life, there is a haunting sense of uncertainty among us.

We have heard the arguments from Scriptures; to some they do not seem to ring with the kind of absolute clarity that drives away all doubts. We recognize that there is a sacredness to the life in the mother's womb, and we find the destruction of that life abhorrent. And yet there are, for most of us, questions about certain circumstances and situations wherein we wonder if abortion is really murder.

What probably complicates the matter even more is that the opposing sides in the debate seem to have cut off the discussion that would help Christians think through the issues involved. To even raise questions or to express doubts over what has become the politically correct posture on abortion is to be declared *persona non grata* in most evangelical circles. It is this inability even to talk about abortion without enduring condemnations and put-downs that adds to all the hurt and confusion that abounds in our midst. Because of this condemnation and confusion, most evangelicals keep their questions to themselves and never go through the kind of reflective process that could help them reach any kind of resolve.

According to one informed source, as many as 20 percent of all abortions are performed on women who claim to be evangelical "born again" Christians. I cannot cite the researcher who gave me that figure because he, himself, is an evangelical Christian, and he told me it would cause him great trouble in his home church if it were known that he had made the statement. He said, "The people in my church hate even the mention of anything about abortion because they wish it were not happening."

We cannot let suppression of honest discussion become a tactic for either side in this debate. We need to talk about this issue with a new openness. The pro-life side must realize that, even if laws are passed making abortions illegal, it would not stop abortions. For that to happen, people would have to be convinced that abortion is wrong. And that is not likely to happen in a climate in which all discussion is cut off out of fear.

The first time I ever asked myself questions about abortion was when my wife was near the time of delivery for our second child. My wife's doctor was Roman Catholic, and that created some uneasiness for me. Whether or not it was true, I had heard that if there are complications in a delivery and a decision has to be made as to whether to save the mother or the baby, a Roman Catholic doctor would work to save the baby.

The matter so troubled me that eventually I met with the doctor and asked him outright: "Doc, if it came to saving either my wife or my baby, which would you choose?"

The doctor sat quietly for a few moments, and then with a

loving, sympathetic, and yet intense look on his face, he threw the question back to me and asked, "What do *you* want me to do?"

I not only thought of myself and my own loss should the baby be chosen over my wife, I thought of my three-year-old daughter and what she would lose if her mother was taken from her. I slowly answered the question: "I would want you to save my wife."

I did not feel comfortable with my answer. Had I crossed the line? Had I abandoned a pro-life stance? Was I on any kind of biblical ground? Was my answer in tune with the will of God?

And so it is that most pro-lifers hold to their position with a degree of humility, if not uncertainty. They sense a rightness about their cause. They are convinced that the life in a mother's womb is sacred and that indiscriminate killing of the unborn is an affront to God. But there is a reluctance to call it murder in all cases. It is this sense of limited ambiguity that pervades the evangelical conscience and keeps many from giving support to killing the doctors at abortion clinics. Most want to leave the ultimate judgments to be made by a higher power.

What makes abortion a particularly difficult issue is that there are some who do not think there are clear-cut biblical references that deal directly with abortion. Those who are strongly pro-life respond to such a claim by saying that in the final analysis the commandment set down by God, "Thou shalt not kill!" should be enough. The problem is that pro-choice proponents argue that this verse refers specifically to killing human beings and then declare that they believe there is little basis for establishing that the fetus *is* a human being.

The pro-life people counter with verses such as these:

Did not he that made me in the womb make him? and did not one fashion us in the womb? (Job 31:15)

For thou hast possessed my reins: thou hast covered me in my mother's womb.

I will praise thee; for I am fearfully and wonderfully made: marvellous are thy works; and that my soul knoweth right well.

My substance was not hid from thee, when I was made
in secret, and curiously wrought in the lowest parts of
the earth.
Thine eyes did see my substance, yet being unperfect;
and in thy book all my members were written, which in
continuance were fashioned, when as yet there was none
of them. (Ps. 139:13–16)

These and other verses, they argue, suggest that God has defined the unborn as persons with spiritual characteristics. Being
known by God as persons is sufficient, they say, to establish the
humanness of the unborn child.

"Not so!" respond the pro-choicers, who will be satisfied with
nothing less than some specific and clear biblical reference that
reads, "Thou shalt not abort the unborn."

The pro-choice argument rests on the assumption that the
unborn fetus has not yet been humanized. I have heard a number of justifications of this assumption; but the one that makes
the most sense to me is that the "humanness" of a person is im-
parted through a relational process. Only the experiencing of
empathetic rapport with another can bring about humanization.
Humanness, according to this argument, is not so much biological inheritance as it is a social interactive process. The pro-choice
people say that during the first eight to ten weeks of embryonic
development, before the developing fetus has an operative brain,
there is no possibility for the kind of interaction between mother
and child that would initiate humanization. Thus, abortion
should be permissible during this early period.

It is further argued by pro-choice advocates that if it were possible to bring an infant *homo sapien* into the world without any
meaningful relationships with humans, then the traits of humanness would never develop in that *homo sapien*. Such a child, like one
raised by wolves, would have only the traits and characteristics of
the creatures that raised it. Such a child, it is contended, would
have no language, no concept of morality, no concept of God, and
no reflective consciousness of being human. Socialization, so this

argument goes, is the means through which a *homo sapien* becomes human.

While this theory has some logic in its favor, there is one flaw to it. And that is that there is increasing evidence that the process of social interaction begins *before* birth. The mother carrying a baby interacts with that unborn child in a variety of meaningful ways, all of which are not yet clear to researchers. If we are to deem the child "human" from the point at which humanizing socialization begins, we will have to give serious attention to what these influences are and how early *in utero* the humanization process begins.

In reality, there are many Christians who remain uncertain on the issue. Many remain unconvinced by either the ardent pro-life or the pro-choice advocates. Neither side has effectively dialogued with this uncommitted group. These confused, undecided Christians have been confronted by protest marches and increasingly strained confrontations with the advocates of both sides. But little light has been shed on the issue to help them make up their minds.

This is an argument in which pro-choice and pro-life people agree on only one thing: that there *is* no middle ground. But ironically, the middle ground is where most Americans, and more specifically, most church members, stand on this issue. In his book *The Battle Over the Family*, Peter Berger, a prominent Lutheran sociologist, makes this point effectively.

Berger suggests that most people who consider themselves pro-choice would object strenuously to permitting abortions in the last month of pregnancy, or for that matter in the last three months of a pregnancy. On the other hand, he contends, a significant proportion of those who call themselves pro-life would reluctantly accept abortions in the earliest stages of pregnancy, especially in cases that involve rape or incest. We would find, says Berger, that among many pro-life Christians there is acceptance of "the morning-after" pills that have been developed in France. Many people in the church, he contends, are strongly pro-life or pro-choice. There is also a silent group that is confused but does not want to discuss the issue because these church people are afraid of the heated argument that would follow.

Berger also claims that many Christians change their opinions on the abortion issue when faced with personal situations in which undesirable pregnancies become problematic. As a case in support of this point, I have a friend who took a very conservative stance on this issue until his daughter had an unwanted pregnancy outside of a marital relationship. Then suddenly, he became a pro-choice supporter.

When all the pros and cons on this issue have been heard, I argue that it is safest to adopt a pro-life position. I argue that since the issue cannot be conclusively decided in either a scientific manner or through Scripture, it is best to chance making an error on the side of life. After all, if one takes a pro-choice position and it is wrong, one will have lent support to the killing of innocent children. Furthermore, all life should be treated as sacred, whether or not it can be determined that in the case of abortion we are dealing with *human* life. I am repulsed by the way in which abortion has come to be treated casually as simply another form of birth control.

But there are women who respond to such logic by saying, "This is the kind of thing we expected to hear from men who do not personally know what an unwanted pregnancy is all about."

I often hear women cry out in anger that men are making decisions that control their biological destinies. They contend that the decision about whether to have an abortion is personal and should be left up to the woman and her doctor.

What such a declaration fails to take into consideration is the strong comeback of the pro-life people. They argue that the unborn fetus is a human being, and therefore abortion constitutes taking a human life. When it comes to murder, they say, it is not up to one human being to determine whether another human being lives or dies. One person cannot be allowed to arbitrarily decide whether another person is entitled to continue to enjoy the life God has given.

As I have addressed this difficult and highly charged subject,

I have tried to maintain some objectivity. I have tried to give dispassionate reflections on a subject that elicits intense passion. I have done this because I wanted each side to gain some feel for the arguments of the other side. We are not going to make any progress toward a consensus on this life-and-death issue unless we understand each other. I know that listening to each other can lead to change because I myself have changed over the years. And I wrote a book on how I have moved toward being pro-life just to show what changed my thinking.

Now, getting back to those militant pro-lifers that shoot up abortion clinics, I have to say that, regardless of any good they *think* they are doing, they are greatly hurting the pro-life cause. The battle over abortion will not be won by bullets. The shooting is only driving the abortion business underground, where it was for years. If people are going to turn away from abortions, it will be because they sense the rightness of doing so. The shootings do nothing to convince anybody of the rightness of the pro-life movement.

In 1950, long before *Roe v. Wade,* the estimate among sociologists was that there were somewhere around three-quarters of a million abortions in America. The law did not allow them, but desperate women figured out ways to get them anyway. Nobody effectively convinced these women that what they were doing was wrong. If pro-lifers have any smarts, they will put the screws on violence and create the conditions where earnest dialogue can take place between the opposing groups of people who are now only shouting at each other.

I think shooting up abortion clinics is not what Jesus would do if He were among us today. And in the end, my ethics always come down to that question: "What would Jesus do?"

11

Was Jesus a Moderate?

JESUS CALLED us into a radical lifestyle. He told His disciples to forsake all and follow Him. He left us no room for lukewarm allegiance. Jesus said if we are lukewarm, He will "spue" us out of His mouth (see Rev. 3:16).

Those of us who have been seduced into the affluent, comfortable, and enjoyable American lifestyle have a hard time facing up to the fact that Jesus said it would be "easier for a camel to go through the eye of a needle, than for a rich man to enter into the kingdom of God" (Matt. 19:24). What Jesus said to the rich young ruler two thousand years ago is meant for the rich young rulers of our generation. If we are to become true disciples of Jesus Christ, we must turn our backs on the wealth, the power, and the prestige that this world so highly values, take up the cross, and follow Jesus (see Matt. 16:24).

Saint Francis of Assisi understood the call of Christ and gave up his comfortable life as a wealthy businessman to take the vows of poverty, chastity, and obedience. He spent his life giving to the poor, keeping nothing for himself.

In our own day, Mother Teresa lives out a similar model of discipleship. She has looked into the eyes of the poor and dying, and she senses that Jesus is looking back at her through those eyes. In response to the presence of Jesus, which Mother Teresa has encountered in the poorest of the poor, she has given all that she could.

The radical lifestyle Jesus expects of His followers is being lived out in the Hutterite communities scattered across the country. Hundreds of Christians have formed themselves into these Christian communities where they live in the simple ways prescribed by Scripture. The Hutterites seek to live out the Sermon on the Mount in their everyday lives. They are pacifists who seek to do good unto all men and women, especially unto those within the household of faith (see Gal. 5:10). The Hutterites try as best they can to reestablish the conditions of the early church, as described in the second chapter of Acts. They hold all possessions in common and share with one another as they find need. The Hutterites endeavor to make their community of Christian brothers and sisters their dominant family. They have their meals and enjoy fellowship as a group rather than in typical American fashion as individual nuclear families.

Whenever I am confronted by the stories of Saint Francis and the examples of Mother Teresa and the Hutterites, I become aware of how much my own life is a compromise with the ways of this world. The very existence of these radically committed Christians forces me to recognize that my salvation had better be by grace through faith, because my works fall far short of what the Bible says the Christian life is all about.

Søren Kierkegaard, the Danish Christian existentialist philosopher, once said, "If we mean by Christian what the New Testament means by Christian, then in any given generation there may be five or six true Christians." He was aware of the radical nature of the lifestyle into which our Lord calls us. Kierkegaard had a hard time accepting the church of his day, because he believed it was so enmeshed with the values of wealth, power, and prestige that mark the secular world.

Kierkegaard told how he once went into the magnificent

cathedral in Copenhagen and took his place in a pew to share in Sunday worship. He recalled how the sun shone through the stained-glass windows and glistened off the brilliantly colored tapestries that hung on the cathedral's walls. He watched as the velvet-robed minister took his place behind the golden pulpit, opened the gilded Bible, marked it with a satin marker, and read, " 'And Jesus said, "If any man would be my disciple, let him forsake all, take up His cross and follow me." ' "

"And," Kierkegaard remarked, "nobody even laughed."

Kierkegaard saw the irony of a church that preaches a Jesus who calls us into a radical lifestyle while itself living comfortably in the ways of the world.

Dietrich Bonhoeffer was another man who understood the radical character of the message of Christ when he declared, "When Jesus calls a man, He bids him come and die." Bonhoeffer lived out such a radical commitment by leaving the safety of America, where he had a prestigious teaching position at Union Theological Seminary in New York, and returning to his native Germany to take his stand against Hitler during World War II.

Bonhoeffer was executed in a Nazi prison camp. He left behind the legacy of a martyr who refused to compromise the radical cost of discipleship.

These saints of the church had a better handle on what the Christian life is supposed to be than most of us do. They understood that Jesus calls us to a radical commitment to the values of the kingdom of God, which He clearly outlined for us in Matthew 5 through 7. When it comes to lifestyle, the call of Christ is a call to radical simplicity, love, and service.

But as radical as the lifestyle prescribed by Christ is, and as wonderfully as He himself perfectly modeled that lifestyle for us, we must also be aware that radical politics was not a thing our Lord embraced or taught. In lifestyle, Jesus was a radical. But when it came to politics, even in its religious forms, He did not embrace the extremism of His day. And in that respect, I think if Jesus were among us in the flesh, He would stand back from the radical politics of our day.

There were radical politics two thousand years ago, as there have been in every era, but Jesus was a member of the Pharisees, a moderate group. To the left of the Pharisees were the Zealots, a party committed to the building of God's kingdom through violence. And to the right of the Pharisees were the Sadducees, who were committed to strict adherence to the Mosaic Law. The Sadducees were the orthodox fundamentalists of their day. They were not about to participate in any foolhardy revolution against the Romans because they believed the Messiah would come to set things right and establish the kingdom. Neither the liberation theology of the Zealots nor the strict orthodoxy of the Sadducees attracted Jesus. He had another way to change the world.

There were other options Jesus could have chosen. If He had really wanted to radically disengage from the Israelite society, as John the Baptist had done, He could have gone out to the desert and joined the Essenes. This extremist group was into holiness in a big way. They considered life in Israel so corrupt that they believed just *living* in the midst of the Jewish society would be spiritually defiling. The followers of the Essene sect withdrew from the worldly ways of Israel and established an isolated community for themselves near the shores of the Dead Sea. There they committed themselves to radical spiritual purity and tried to live out the laws of God without any compromises with the sinful world outside.

Jesus is not into such radical separation from society. He is a God who moves into the neighborhoods where we common people live and work. He is a Savior who chooses to be among people whose hands are dirty with the affairs of everyday life. Radical disengagement from the ebb and flow of life in the cultural mainstream was not the life He modeled for His followers.

Another option for Jesus would have been to make Himself one with the Herodians. They were people who called themselves radically relevant. They saw who held political power, and they came to terms with them. They recognized the risks that go with becoming part of the ruling establishment, but they believed these risks had to be taken if anything significant was going to get done.

The Herodians believed that real religion required that they became the radical incarnation of the dominant socioeconomic system. They were the ones who made the case that the only way to change things was to work within the established order and do what was possible within its constraints. Some will say the Herodians sold out. Their answer would be that they made the sacrifice those who would be realistic must make if progress toward the kingdom of God is going to be achieved.

Jesus undoubtedly knew about all of these political parties and was well versed in their ideologies. But in the end, He was not about to be swept into any of them. Instead, He identified with the Pharisees, because their theology was closest to the message He had come to declare.

The Pharisees took the Scriptures seriously but were not into the rigid orthodoxy of the Sadducees. They were Jews who affirmed the traditions of the past but were also open to new truths God was making known to His people.

Jesus was very much with the Pharisees when it came to a firm doctrine of a life after death. He, like His fellow Pharisees, taught that when this life is over, there is a judgment day and a promise of eternal life. In this, Jesus was at odds with the radical fundamentalism of the Sadducees, who would not accept these truths because Moses had not written about such things in the only books of the Bible they accepted.

Like the Pharisees, Jesus stood for maintaining the basic message of Scripture. He warned that the souls of those who tamper with or try to change that basic message are in danger (see Rev. 22:18–19). But, unlike the Pharisees, Jesus was against the way many of them had embroidered the original texts of the Bible. He found in their additions to the Word of God a host of burdensome legalisms that weighed down the faithful.

As I read the New Testament, I find, as most Bible scholars do, sufficient evidence that Jesus was indeed a Pharisee. However, I have to add that He was nominal in His membership in this leading Jewish denomination even though He undoubtedly held theological beliefs that established His religious identity in the school of the Pharisees. You cannot read the story of Jesus without being aware of His persistent criticism of them. He was constantly on their case because, while their theology may have been sound, they seemed to major in minors. He saw them as religious people who were more concerned about checking out the theological implications of every word and deed than they were in expressing the love of God. And it is the *love* of God that the *laws* of God are all about (see Matt. 22:34–40).

Jesus did not mind being religious, but what He really did was to make it clear that something more than religion (even the religion of the Pharisees, which He Himself embraced) would be required of those who would be part of the kingdom of God.

> For I say unto you, That except your righteousness shall exceed the righteousness of the scribes and Pharisees, ye shall in no case enter into the kingdom of heaven. (Matt. 5:20)

What Jesus did was to make being right with God a matter of relationships rather than a matter of living out the rituals and regulations of a particular religious sect or denomination. He taught, ever so clearly, that to relate to God with passionate love is what is of ultimate significance. Jesus went on to say that tied up with loving God with all of one's heart, mind, soul, and strength is loving the people around us with that same passionate intensity.

Instead of looking for God in the temples and churches of this or that denomination or religion, Jesus taught us to look for Him when we look into the eyes of the poor and oppressed. According to His words to us, God is known not in religion but in relationships with those whom the world calls "the least of these my brethren" (Matt. 25:40). Jesus warns that those who trust in religion rather than in a personal relationship with Him and with those needy people who want to be loved in His name may be in for some painful surprises on the day of judgment.

> Lord, when saw we thee an hungered, or athirst, or a stranger, or naked, or sick, or in prison, and did not minister unto thee?
> Then shall he answer them, saying, Verily I say unto you, Inasmuch as ye did it not to one of the least of these, ye did it not to me. And these shall go away into everlasting punishment: but the righteous into life eternal. (Matt. 25:44–46)

Jesus may have been a Pharisee in the sense that this was His denominational affiliation, but it was not in the religious mind-set of the Pharisees that He offered us His salvation. Nor could His salvation be found in the more radical religious sects and movements of His day. Salvation can be had only in knowing Him and loving Him as he comes to us through the lost and the least and the last of all the people we encounter.

There are always people looking to some radical religion for their hope and deliverance. The Jesus who called people to look beyond religion and to radically love one another in His name is not to their liking. Jesus' enemies much preferred radical religion to radical love, and that is why they crucified Him.

The tale is told that two thousand years ago there lived in the small town of Nazareth two boys named Jesus. The name Jesus was not unusual back there and then, even as it is not unusual in Hispanic communities today. The name means "deliverer" or "savior."

One Jesus, according to this story, had a father named Abbas, and hence was known as "Jesus Bar-Abbas"—"Bar" meaning "son of." The other Jesus had a father named Joseph and therefore was called "Jesus Bar-Joseph."

Each of these boys had a special charisma. Each talked about seeing the kingdom of God made real in history. Each stood out from the other boys. In the small synagogue where they studied the Torah, one might suppose that the rabbi might easily have confused them. They were somewhat alike, and yet there was a world of difference between them. Jesus Barabbas saw the hope of Israel in a violent revolution that would drive out the horrid Romans. The other Jesus talked about a kingdom created by radically loving people—and even about radically loving one's enemies.

As they grew up, these two boys went their separate ways. One Jesus organized a radical religious movement that would do whatever was necessary, including killing and stealing, to create his utopian kingdom. The other Jesus seemed to shy away from political power, even when the crowd hailed Him as the Messiah before the Passover feast one year and wanted to crown Him king.

These two men named Jesus were destined to meet again. It would be in Pilate's court. The one, who had become a member of a radical religious sect called the Zealots, would be accused of being a murdering thief. And in truth, his radical revolution had made him into one.

The other Jesus would be accused simply of "stirring up the people," which indeed He had done. Yet Pilate found no fault in this second Jesus. He sensed in Him something other-worldly and good. He would have released Him except for the fact that doing so would have been such bad politics.

The second Jesus had made a lot of religious people angry because He took their religion so lightly. He talked about God in ways that went beyond their religion, even in its most radical forms. The religious people despised Him for that because their religion was all they had.

And so Pilate did what many politicians have done and still choose to do, right down to the present day. Instead of voting his conscience, Pilate voted his constituency. He polled the populace.

Politicians are always taking polls before making decisions. He asked the people which Jesus they wanted released to them. And the crowd cried . . . "Barabbas."

The crowd always prefers a radical religion to a radical lifestyle of loving sacrifice. The Jesus they wanted to crucify was a moderate only when it came to religion. He was radical about something far more important.

12

Should Christians Support Gun Control?

IT ALL BOILS down to a matter of rights. The Bill of Rights guarantees every American the *right* to bear arms, but the Constitution does not specify what kind of arms. When Congress tries to encroach on this right by prohibiting first one kind of gun and then another, there *is* justification for Americans to stand up and yell, "They're taking away our rights!"

There can be no argument about the fact that groups like the National Rifle Association have the law on their side and are simply upholding an American tradition. Nor can there be much argument against the claim that now, more than ever, Americans have a need to defend themselves. With violent crime as extensive as it is, it is easy to make the case that Americans need to ensure their own self-defense by possessing guns.

Recently, I watched and listened to some of the congressional testimony on gun control on C-Span. A committee was considering new legislation on guns, and the NRA brought as witnesses a number of people who might have been dead had they not had automatic weapons to defend themselves. One man spoke of having used a machine gun to fend off a gang that threatened to invade his remotely located recreational cabin. The automatic attack weapon that he claimed had saved his life was a gun which, according to laws that had just been put on the books, could no longer be manufactured. Granted, his case was extremely unusual, but it is still a fact that if he had not been able to have that "attack weapon," who knows what would have happened to him?

The other side of the argument is also commonly known. The streets of urban America have become battlefields. Teenagers are packing guns with such awesome firepower that the bullets are able to penetrate the so-called "bulletproof" vests the police wear for protection. Across the country, police officers are being outgunned in the shootouts that have become far too common in our country. Police chiefs in every major city (who are hardly known for their liberal politics!) are pleading for changes in the law so that restrictions are placed on who can own guns as well as on the kinds of guns that can be sold.

It is increasingly obvious that more and more guns are getting into the hands of those who lack the maturity or emotional stability to use them responsibly. This became abundantly clear when Colin Ferguson, an obviously psychotic man, was legally able to buy an automatic weapon in the morning and then use it to shoot up a couple dozen innocent people on a Long Island commuter train that afternoon.

There are no tests or regulations that could have prohibited this crazy man from buying that gun. There are no regulations on purchases of firearms that could have prevented such a tragedy from happening. In reality, there are more controls over who can and cannot get a driver's license than there are over who can and cannot get a gun.

The NRA has systematically and consistently lobbied lawmakers to prevent any kind of restraints on gun ownership or any method of licensing the people who own guns. It is no secret that the NRA is among the biggest and best-financed lobbying groups around; it exercises far more influence than the size of its membership would suggest. Most lawmakers are anxious to vote in ways that please the NRA, despite surveys and polls that show that most

Americans want some form of gun control and licensing of own-
ers. This just goes to show what effective lobbying and a lot of
money can accomplish. One critical commentator remarked,
"When it comes to gun control, nobody should complain about
the U.S. Congress because it is the best Congress money can buy."

When I say that guns are falling into the hands of many who
lack the maturity to handle them responsibly, I need only to
allude to statistics to support my case. A recent analysis of
schoolchildren's behavior showed that one out of ten children
had carried weapons (often guns) to school with them at one
time or another. Furthermore, one out of fourteen schoolchildren had been threatened by schoolmates wielding weapons.

In a town just north of where I live, a high school student shot
to death a classmate who had been picking on him. The shooting took place in the chemistry lab in full view of all the others
in the class. Do not such things suggest that some kind of regulations and controls are needed?

Another fact that has to be considered is that most murders
are committed by family members in their own homes, usually
late at night. Many times, people who are tired and stressed out
kill their spouses, parents, and/or children only to go into deep
remorse a few hours later. Others, under the influence of drugs
or alcohol, commit murders they cannot even remember when
they become sober. Isn't there something wrong when guns are
so readily accessible to such troubled people?

And then there is the matter of the kinds of guns that remain
uncontrolled. When we talk about "attack weapons," we mean
guns that have no other possible use than the killing of people.
These are heavy-duty guns that fall into the category of machine
guns and even bazookas. Such guns have no viability for hunting.
They would blow the game—even large game—to smithereens.
Do ordinary citizens really need bullets that can pierce armor?
And what about that stubby little revolver nicknamed "the Satur-
day night special"? It is cheap to buy, and its primary use has
been for armed robbery.

In response to all these facts, the gun protagonists contend that if owning guns becomes criminal, than only criminals will have guns. After all, they logically argue, if laws are passed to control who can own guns and what kinds of guns can be owned, criminals would not be likely to obey such laws. They say that people who want guns to break the law probably would break any laws established to regulate guns. So why make things tough on good people when gun control will have no effect on bad people?

This debate is not likely to be resolved in the foreseeable future because there is something to be said about the validity of the cases on both sides. But Christians have to look at the question of gun control from another point of view. Specifically, Christians have to look to the Bible and ask what Scriptures have to say about all of this. There will be those who respond to this by saying, "Just a minute! The Bible doesn't speak to the issue of gun control. As a matter of fact, guns didn't even exist in Bible times."

All of that may be true. But the Bible does lay down some basic principles that can be applied to just about every question and issue of our modern times. In this case, we ought to consider what the Bible says about the issue of exercising one's rights, even when doing so can have dire consequences for "weaker" brothers and sisters.

Almost two thousand years ago, the apostle Paul addressed a situation in the city of Corinth, and what he said back then is relevant to our discussion of gun control. That situation had to do with the eating of meats that had been offered to idols.

The early Christians were faced with an interesting dilemma. When it came to getting a good bargain in food, there were few better deals than buying meat that had been previously sacrificed to idols as part of the pagan worship of the day. Once the religious ceremonies were over, the animal was taken from the pagan altar and its meat was sold in the public marketplace. Many Christians in Corinth, knowing a good deal when they saw it, would buy the meat. They probably thought they were practicing good Christian stewardship.

Personally, Paul could see nothing wrong with buying and eating meats that had been offered to idols. From his perspective, the very existence of idols was just an evil joke. Paul did not see any point in letting a good steak go to waste just because it had sat for a few minutes in front of a make-believe deity carved out of stone.

The problem was with some of the pious legalists in the Corinthian congregation. In every congregation in every era there have always been those religious types who diminish the freedom others have in Christ by laying guilt trips on them. These are the ones who look for little things they can label as "unspiritual" or "worldly" and make them into controversial matters for the church. Because of these "weaker brothers and sisters," as Paul called them, certain nonissues became crucial matters of faith and practice. Stumbling over these minor issues, Paul said, caused some to lose sight of what the gospel is all about. Even today, certain religious types can get so worked up over these petty arguments that they have no energy left to live out the gospel or even to understand what the Christian lifestyle is all about. In response to these weaker brothers and sisters, Paul wrote:

> As concerning therefore the eating of those things that are offered in sacrifice unto idols, we know that an idol is nothing in the world, and that there is none other God but one.
> For though there be that are called gods, whether in heaven or in earth, (as there be gods many, and lords many,) but to us there is but one God, the Father, of whom are all things, and we in him; and one Lord Jesus Christ, by whom are all things, and we by him.
> Howbeit, there is not in every man that knowledge: for some with conscience of the idol unto this hour eat it as a thing offered unto an idol; and their conscience being weak is defiled.

But meat commendeth us not to God; for neither, if we eat, are we the better; neither, if we eat not, are we the worse.

But take heed lest by any means this liberty of yours become a stumblingblock to them that are weak.

For if any man see thee which hast knowledge sit at meat in the idol's temple, shall not the conscience of him which is weak be emboldened to eat those things which are offered to idols; and through thy knowledge shall the weak brother perish, for whom Christ died?

But when ye sin so against the brethren, and wound their weak conscience, ye sin against Christ.

Wherefore, if meat make my brother to offend, I will eat no flesh while the world standeth, lest I make my brother to offend. (1 Cor. 8:4–13)

Paul is willing to forego rights if it will save those who can't handle those rights. He lets it be known that as a Christian living under the grace of God it is "lawful" for him to eat the meats offered to idols, but he adds that for him it is no big deal one way or the other (see 1 Cor. 6:12). Consequently, he said he would refrain from eating the controversial meat in order to spare his weaker brothers and sisters from something that could keep them from getting close to God and something that could hurt the peace of the church. That is what Paul meant in 1 Cor. 6:12 when he wrote, "All things are lawful unto me, but all things are not expedient."

I think what Paul said about meats offered to idols two thousand years ago can be a basis for what I chose to do about guns here and now. I certainly have the *right* to own a gun. The Constitution guarantees me that right, as I pointed out earlier. But perhaps, as a Christian, I should forego my right for the sake of weaker brothers and sisters. Maybe I should *choose* to establish and obey a law I know is needed by those who cannot handle too much freedom with guns. Shouldn't Christians be willing to give up their rights on nonessential things in order to secure what is good for others? Is that what Christian love requires?

Allow me to suggest that Christians ought to model a lifestyle with respect to guns that weaker brothers and sisters can follow without getting into trouble. Permit me to say to the church that, given what is going on in society today, Christians need to give up their weapons so that those who cannot handle weapons responsibly might follow our example.

I want to challenge Christians to accept as a principle that, insofar as it is reasonable, the strong and able ought to so live and regulate their lives that, in following them, the weak and irresponsible will be safe and saved. If that means I have to give up some of my rights, so be it.

I believe that what I am suggesting as a principle for Christians in the matter of gun control would be a good idea to guide society at large. We need to create a world in which the weak are protected.

Unfortunately, it is not always possible for such a clear and simple principle to be applied in a simple manner. I would like to see the matter of weapon control handled without people losing the right to use guns to hunt *for food*. I also recognize that self-defense is a serious concern that may, in some cases, warrant the possession of a gun. But perhaps, in the latter case, I ought to listen to my Anabaptist brothers and sisters who call me to a pacifism I find difficult to accept. Many of my Mennonite and Hutterite brothers and sisters tell me I should trust in God for protection, rather than in guns. And they tell me we should be ready to yield to the evil others would do to us rather than harm them. I have not gotten to that place yet, but I am on my way. My pacifist friends put me under great conviction when they ask me the simple question, "If Jesus were among us in the flesh, would He pack a gun—even if He had to walk through a dangerous neighborhood?" And if I answer, as I am prone to do, "I don't think so, . . ." they follow up by asking, "Are not Christians people who do what Jesus would do if He were in their place?"

13

Is Christian Environmentalism an Oxymoron?

NOW THAT WE don't have the Communists to kick around anymore, we evangelicals have begun to make the environmentalists the main players in our conspiracy theories. I have heard sermons go so far as to claim that the environmentalist causes are nothing more than a disguise for the New Age movement and that the whole thing is demonically inspired.

Less-extreme criticism has focused on the cost of environmental regulations to the American public in general and to business and industry in particular. Politically conservative critics, who usually are highly respected by evangelical Christians, constantly point out that environmentalism is just one more foolhardy cause of the liberal political establishment that is costing Americans jobs on the one hand while hindering our economic growth on the other.

Even among those evangelical Christians who are not especially antagonistic toward the environmentalist movement there is general apathy toward environmentalist issues. Recent studies indicate that the more evangelical the theology of people, the less likely they are to show concern for protecting the earth from a possible ecological disaster. It seems as though the more committed Christians become to the ministries of evangelical churches, the less committed they are to saving the environment from pollution and from unbridled exploitation of nonrenewable national resources.

Those who see the environmental movement as a New Age thing can make a good case for their claim. There is no doubt that the New Age movement has hijacked environmentalism and tried to make it their own special cause. This attempted takeover has not been difficult, given the indifference of evangelicals to the plight of the environment and the ways in which we have usually reacted to legislation that would protect our national habitat. It is just about impossible to go to a conference on the environment without hearing speeches about the spiritual qualities of nature delivered in New Age language. I know of seminars held during conferences on the environment that taught New Age religion as a way of life that could save the planet from destruction.

Adding to this problem is the trend in many environmentalist get-togethers of promoting New Age religion while putting down the Christian faith. Among the most popular essays circulated among environmentalists is "The Historical Roots of Our Ecological Crisis" by Lynn White, which puts a huge amount of the blame for the environmental problems of our time on the teachings of Reformed theologian John Calvin. According to White, it was the Calvinistic doctrine, which teaches that we humans have been given dominion over nature, that gave rise to the destructive attitudes toward nature that now characterize our society. White says it was Calvin who contended that God gave us the right to exploit nature for our own purposes and to enhance our own wealth and well-being. This, he says, is what has given rise to the guiltless ways in which people have sought to get rich while using up natural resources, obliterating the beauty of God's creation and threatening the ecological balance of the planet. Having many of the environmentalists feel this way about Christianity has hardly endeared their movement to evangelicals.

All of this troubles me deeply because I am convinced that being committed to saving the environment is both a Christian calling and a social responsibility. There are good reasons why we Christians must change our attitudes and take back from the New Agers what really should be a Christian concern. The reality is that it is a concern of urgent importance.

First of all, as Christians, we ought to be concerned about what our abuse of the environment is going to mean to ourselves and to our own health. Personally, I am convinced that the incredible increase in the incidence of cancer today is related to what we have been doing to nature. To start with, there is growing evidence that our use of hydrocarbons has been releasing into the upper levels of the atmosphere an array of chemicals that are eating away at the ozone layer which protects us from the harmful ultraviolet rays of the sun. The diminishing ability of the ozone layer to act as a filter means that harmful rays that can cause skin cancer are getting through to us.

There are other ways in which our health is being adversely affected because of our abuse of nature. More and more evidence points to the fact that chemicals we are using for fertilizer are getting into our bodies by way of the food we eat. Some of these chemicals have a cancerous effect and pose a variety of other health hazards.

All of these examples are short-term effects of our irresponsible stewardship of nature. The long-term effects will have to be endured by our children and our children's children. Scientists are warning us about the effects of global warming. Because of the carbon monoxide we are constantly pumping into the air, a layer of gas is forming in the upper atmosphere that creates what has been called "the greenhouse effect." Quite simply, what is happening is that the light of the sun gets through and hits the earth's surface, generating heat. This heat is supposed to rise and dissipate into outer space. But now the layer of gas formed by carbon monoxide and other gases traps some of the heat and keeps it within our atmosphere. The cumulative results of this trapping of heat have caused gradual increases in the tempera-ture, which, in turn, are bringing about significant changes in the earth's climate and weather.

Scientists are discovering that glaciers in the polar regions are now showing signs of melting because of global warming. Some are predicting that it will not be long before the abun-dance of water this produces will raise the level of the oceans. Large, heavily populated areas along the shores will then be underwater. As the warming effect continues, areas that are now temperate will become tropical, and tropical areas will tend toward desertification.

Our great-grandchildren could end up living in a world in which New York City has palm trees lining the Hudson River and Phoenix has weeks of temperatures over 120 degrees. Nations like Bangladesh would cease to exist in this future because tor-rential rains and rising floods would have killed off millions of people and driven others to seek higher ground in Pakistan and India. Entire nations would experience massive immigration because of climate changes.

Beyond the effects of climate and weather, we have to con-sider other problems we will leave behind because of our irresponsible lifestyles. What respiratory illnesses will our great-grandchildren suffer because of what we have done to the atmosphere? How much will the aesthetic fulfillment of their lives be diminished because of the destruction of beauty that ac-companies our rape of the earth's surface?

As the environment suffers, we will find that our capacity to produce the food necessary for the expanding human family will diminish. Deforestation and the soil erosion that quickly follows it have already reduced the food-production capacities of such nations as Haiti and Bangladesh. Only massive food supplies being shipped in from the outside can sustain the people in these countries. Weather changes caused by the destruction of rain forests are already affecting poor people all over the world.

During a trip to Africa, I visited with a tribal chief whose people lived along the Senegal River just south of Mauritania. His nomadic tribe was dying out. A prolonged drought had been responsible for the death of the herds of goats that for generations had provided their livelihood. Young people in growing numbers were leaving tribal life for the city of Dakar in hope of finding some means of survival. There was no doubt in the chief's mind that his people were facing extinction.

When I asked this tribal chief what could be done, he shrugged his shoulders and said, "Nothing!"

"This is not a drought," he explained. "We have had droughts before. My people know how to live through droughts. The world is changing! All the land is turning into desert, and there can be no future for us when that happens."

This chief had no scholarly background in meteorology or geography, but he knew in ways that transcend the ways of our science that something cataclysmic was happening to the environment. He did not have the facts scientists have at their disposal, but he knew something had gone wrong with his world. Scientists could tell him that rain forests in Brazil and in other places are being destroyed at a rate that startles the imagination, and that as these rain forests vanish from the earth the weather patterns, which they dramatically influence, are significantly altered. Scientists could also tell him these weather changes are part of what is causing the expansion of the Sahara Desert southward over the continent of Africa. According to one reliable estimate, the Sahara is moving south at the rate of two miles a year. Scientists would join the African chief in asking, How long will it be before the poor people of Africa are left with no land to support them?

As Christians, we should be deeply disturbed by the reports of world hunger. From the Scriptures we should know that feeding the hungry is one of the most important obligations for Christ's followers. Our concern for the hungry should drive us to be environmentally concerned. If our own destruction of nature diminishes the ability of the earth to yield food, then poor people will starve in greater and greater numbers. At present, according to *Compassion International*, more than forty thousand children in this world die *daily* from starvation and disease related to malnutrition. How many more will be dying from these causes a decade from now?

There is yet another reason for being environmentally concerned that is seldom considered in our discussions about rescuing nature. It is the way our destruction of the earth's beauty and our annihilation of many species of animals, insects, and plant life impact the worship of God. In our self-centeredness, we are prone to think that only we human beings have the capacity or the urge to worship the Creator. But the Bible is quite clear that all of nature was created for this purpose.

To most of us in Western Christianity, worship is not a primary part of our religion. We are activists, and we tend to believe that what God really wants from His people is for them to give loving service to the poor and oppressed. While this activistic dimension of our faith is certainly supported by huge numbers of scriptural texts, we must not forget that, in an ultimate sense, God created us and saved us for His own honor and glory. Furthermore, not only were we made for the worship of God, so was all of nature. The Bible calls upon nature to join us in worshiping Him.

> Praise ye the LORD. Praise ye the LORD from the heavens: praise him in the heights.
> Praise ye him, all his angels; praise ye him all his hosts.
> Praise ye him, sun and moon: praise him, all ye stars of light.
> Praise him, ye heavens of heavens, and ye waters that be above the heavens.
> Let them praise the name of the LORD: for he commanded, and they were created. (Ps. 148:1–5)

Everything that was created was ordained to glorify God and to worship Him. Obviously, not all creatures are capable of responding to the awesomeness of God in the same manner. Each species has its own unique way of reflecting God's glory and lifting up praise to Him. The level of self-consciousness and the kind of awareness evident in creatures varies widely from species to species. But each, in its own way, was ordained to reflect the glory of God and to magnify His name in worship.

One of my friends mockingly called me an evangelist who was out to save the whales. I explained to him that, while my primary obligation as an evangelist was to tell other people about what Jesus had done for them, I also feel obliged to do just what he said: save the whales.

Those who are into the Bible should realize that whales, which in Scripture are called the "leviathans" of the deep, are special creations of God (see, for example, Job 14:1). The songs they sing (and yes, humpback whales do sing) are hymns meant for God. If there were no humans on the planet, there would still be a purpose for whales—to worship God and to glorify Him forever (see Ps. 148:7).

It is very hard for most Americans to grasp what worship is all about. We are too utilitarian in our approach to life to easily comprehend the idea that praise directed toward God has ultimate meaning in and of itself. But all of this changes when a person is filled with the Holy Spirit. The indwelling presence of the Spirit creates within us an impulse to pour out songs and shouts of praise to the Lord. It is then that we are able, as the old hymn suggests, to "join with all nature in manifold witness" to the glory of our God.

Once we grasp the significance of worship and gain some insight into the role of nature in worship, we can understand why saving the whales is so important. Humpback whales sing songs, flying fish leap from the sea, eagles soar in glorious circles in the sky, tiny flowers and fluttering butterflies add bright splashes of color, and giant redwoods stand in reverent silence. God made them all for His glory, each to praise Him in its own way.

What has been said about saving whales also can be said about preserving other creatures. To be sure, some have not the intelligence of whales, but each in its own way is meant to glorify the Lord. Plants and insects, too, have their place in the scheme of cosmic worship.

Saint Francis of Assisi once called on the crickets to chirp music for their Maker. On another occasion he called on the sheep of the fields to lift their voices and "bah" unto the Lord. If you call Saint Francis crazy, you may be making a confession rather than an accusation. For in what you say, you only reveal how far you are removed from saintly spirituality.

If Saint Francis were among us today, I am sure he would be an environmentalist. He saw in all nature the glory of God, and he wanted to preserve each part of it for that purpose God intended. In his spirituality, Saint Francis undoubtedly would have preached the biblical mandate to rescue nature from its present painful condition. I am sure he would preach to us from Paul's writings, reminding us that the world's most famous evangelist since Christ has called upon us to rescue creation.

> For the earnest expectation of the creature waiteth for the manifestation of the sons of God.
> For the creature was made subject to vanity, not willingly, but by reason of him who had subjected the same in hope, because the creature itself also shall be delivered from the bondage of corruption into the glorious liberty of the children of God.
> For we know that the whole creation groaneth and travaileth in pain together until now. (Rom. 8:19–22)

To my Pentecostal friends, I want to say in no uncertain terms that being filled with the Holy Spirit, which is what this eighth chapter of Romans is all about, involves commitment to saving creation from evil destruction. Being filled with the Spirit is to wrestle with those principalities and powers that are doing evil with nature.

That is why Christian environmentalism is not an oxymoron. Being Christian and being environmentally concerned go together. The latter is an expression of the former.

Some Christians have gotten together to carry out the mandate to save creation by forming the Christian Environmental Association. This organization has a broad commitment to educating other Christians about what they should be doing to rescue God's creation from the exploitative irresponsibility of the human race. In addition to the seminars, retreats, and study tours it conducts for educational purposes, CEA has a strong commitment to some projects that give concrete expression to it's overall mission.

The first project is to buy up a rain forest in Belize. Instead of just hurling invectives at those who are destroying this nonrenewable resource, CEA is buying and preserving as many acres of rain forest as it can. The organization presently has an option to buy some of it at one hundred dollars an acre and has already lined up scores of people to put up money to start the purchasing. One of the things that makes this project so attractive is that it is the sort of thing that can involve a church youth group or a Sunday school class. Groups such as these can easily come up with one hundred dollars. Many concerned individuals can afford an investment like this also. For one hundred dollars, an acre of the rain forest is saved and the group or individual gets a certificate verifying the purchase to hang on the wall. The founders of CEA are convinced that protest marches and petition signing are not going to change much. But *buying* the rain forest is one sure way of getting this vital part of God's creation out of the hands of those who would destroy it.

The second major program of the Christian Environmental Association is an attempt to impact what goes on at Earth Day celebrations. Each year in cities across the country, environmentally concerned people get together to celebrate nature and call for responsible care of our natural habitat. As you can well imagine, these get-togethers are bonanzas for New Age religionists. You can count on them showing up with their crystals and their mystical chants. But CEA does not take this as a reason to retreat from Earth Day celebrations. Instead, this group takes God's Word at face value when it says, "Resist the devil, and he will flee from you" (James 4:7b).

Those in the Christian environmentalist movement intend to be highly visible at these gatherings, holding forth a witness for Christ. Their message is a modification of the famous Four Spiritual Laws outlined by Bill Bright of Campus Crusade. They tell the others at the Earth Day celebrations that if they love creation, they ought to want to meet the Creator. Their tract tells the reader:

1. God has a wonderful plan for you and His creation.

2. Sin has ruined God's plan.

3. God sent His Son Jesus into the world so that both you and all of His creation can be restored to what He planned for both to be.

4. By acknowledging Jesus as Lord and Savior of your life you can join with Him to be personally renewed and to renew all of creation.

These Christian environmentalists do not want to destroy the Earth Day celebration. Instead, they want to save it from pagan influences so it can be an instrument of God for rescuing nature. They want to evangelize nonChristian environmentalists rather than condemn them.

Heresies arise when a truth of God is neglected. Some group comes along, picks up that neglected truth, and twists it into a lie that resembles the truth just enough to attract people. Satan always deceives by distorting truth in this manner. Christians must be ready to rescue the truth from its distorted form and make it part of "the whole counsel of God." As Christians get involved in environmental issues, it is crucial that they make sure the truth the environmental movement embodies is differentiated from the distortions the New Age movement creates. Here are some simple rules to remember:

1. Nature is not to be worshiped. Nature is not God. God is "totally other" than nature. God holds nature together, but

He is outside of nature, and His Word calls any worship of nature "idolatry" (see Rom. 1:23).

2. Human beings are infinitely more precious to God than all the rest of nature. There is "a great chain of being." That means there is a hierarchy in nature, and humans are placed above all else in God's creation. There is a spirituality to humans that is unique, and it is primarily for our salvation that Christ went to the cross.

3. In this hierarchy of life, there is nothing wrong with sacrificing lower forms of life in order to sustain higher forms of life. Vegetarianism may be a good idea, but it is not a biblical mandate for this present age.

Perhaps it is time for you to overcome your fear of being a Christian environmentalist. If you want to join the Christian Environmental Association, write to:

THE CHRISTIAN ENVIRONMENTAL ASSOCIATION
1650 Zanker Road, Suite 150
San Jose, California 95112

Another organization you could also consider if you want to become involved in the environmentalist movement on Christian terms is Green Cross, which has been created by Evangelicals for Social Action. The address of this group is:

GREEN CROSS
10 Lancaster Avenue
Wynwood, Pennsylvania 19096

Do not wait. If you sense a leading of the Lord to make creation care a part of your ministry, follow through right now. This is a movement in which immediate action is crucial. Every day we are losing ground to destructive forces that threaten

God's creation. Now is the accepted time; today is the day of salvation—not only for us as individuals, but for all that is in God's world.

14

Do Christians Have a Right
to Take Over America?

IN MY YOUNGER days, I often urged young people to join together and start a movement to take over America. I could always
arouse an audience of teenagers and young adults by shouting
out that there was enough potential in the auditorium to take
over the nation if they would just commit themselves, without res-
ervations, to the cause.

At the heart of my message was the claim that Jesus had come
into the world to start a revolution, and that to become a Christian was to become an agent of that revolution and to participate
with Him in His great purposes for history. I told my audiences
that when God created the kingdoms of this world He willed for
them to be societies marked by love and justice. I explained that
it was not His will for there to be grinding poverty and massive
hunger. Nor was it His will that the humanity of any people be
diminished through political oppression, racial discrimination,
sexism, or militarism.

I called on my listeners to join with God and be part of a
movement that would change the kingdoms of this world into
the kingdom of our God. I told people that to be Christian was
to participate with the Holy Spirit in making Jesus Christ the

Lord of all things, both in heaven and on earth. There was a solid biblical foundation for what I preached. The apostle Paul called us to such a mission:

> And [God] hath put all things under [Christ's] feet, and gave him to be the head over all things to the church. (Eph. 1:22)

An unbiased reading of the Gospels will leave no doubt that Jesus came to establish His kingdom here on earth. Each of the first three Gospels has Him initiating His ministry with the simple declaration that we should repent because the kingdom of God is at hand.

> From that time Jesus began to preach, and to say, "Repent: for the kingdom of heaven is at hand." (Matt. 4:17)

When Jesus taught His disciples to pray, He taught them to pray, "Thy kingdom come. Thy will be done in earth, as it is in heaven" (Matt. 6:10). His parables were teachings about the coming kingdom of God. Jesus compared what would happen when the kingdom comes to what would happen to bridesmaids who are unprepared for a wedding, and to a certain sower who went forth to sow, and to wheat and tares growing up together, and to leaven, and to a mustard seed.

The list of Jesus' parables about the kingdom of God goes on and on. And when He was about to leave this world and ascend to sit on the right hand of His Father, the last thing Jesus did was to go over, for one last time, His teachings concerning the kingdom of God (see Matthew 25).

My emphasis on the kingdom of God, in my early preaching days, made my usually evangelical audiences very aware of the social dimensions of the gospel. For the most part, my listeners were people who had been raised on a gospel that focused on individualistic salvation. They had been led to view Christianity as a means through which people could have a fulfilling existence in this life and also prepare for the "main event," which will come after this life on earth was over.

My emphasis on the kingdom of God got my listeners to pay attention to the societal dimensions of the Christian faith. It helped them see the legitimacy of what many had disparagingly called "the social gospel." The Jesus I preached called us not only to win individuals into a personal saving relationship to Christ but also to be at work trying to transform society into what His father willed it to be. My message was always, in part, a call to action.

Others have heralded this same message. My good friend Ron Sider founded Evangelicals for Social Action (ESA) with the same goal in mind. He wanted Christians to recognize that they have a responsibility to enter into the political debates of our time and to work for the kind of legislation that expresses "kingdom values." Sider, along with many other progressive evangelicals, has deplored the ways in which evangelicals in the past have disengaged from politics because they believed social action belonged to the agenda of theological liberals.

Well, things have certainly changed! Over the past twenty years, evangelicals have been shaken into an awareness of their social responsibilities, and they are now wide awake to the calling to impact the American political system with their votes and their hard work. The wake-up call to change America came largely in reaction to the *Roe v. Wade* ruling by the Supreme Court and also because of some of the things that happened with the election of Jimmy Carter.

For most evangelicals, the ruling that made abortion legal in America was all the evidence they needed that secular humanism was overtaking the nation. That ruling convinced them that America, which they had once believed to be a Christian nation, was going down the tubes. They believed that true Christians had to take their stand against the godless trends that were now evident everywhere. With the *Roe v. Wade* ruling on abortion, they were convinced that secular humanists, particularly the ones who were feminists, had gone too far and had to be stopped.

The situation became even more alarming for many evangelicals shortly after Jimmy Carter was elected president. Carter, in accord with one of his campaign promises, called the White House Conference on the Family. Being convinced that many of the most troublesome problems of our society could be traced to the disintegration of the family, Carter hoped his administration could do something to revitalize family life in America. To that end, he brought together "experts" in the field of family studies, making sure the opinions and values of our diverse population were represented.

What came out of the White House Conference on the Family was a political nightmare for Carter. It created an intense reaction that, in many ways, is responsible for much of what is going on in America today. The most upsetting result of the conference was a non-result. The conferees could agree on very little, but what was most disturbing to politically conservative evangelicals was that the conferees could not even come up with a clear definition of what was a family. There were those who argued that couples living together outside of wedlock should be considered families. There were others who contended that teenage unwed mothers and their children should be labeled as "normative families." But what really set the sparks flying was when the claim was made that co-habitating gay and lesbian couples be recognized as legitimate family units. That was just too much for most evangelical Christians to accept with any grace.

Along with their concern over abortion, this issue convinced evangelicals that there were anti-Christian forces at work in Washington that were attacking traditional family values. They were further convinced that they had to do something about it. They believed they had to take America back from the secular humanists who were ruining it and try to make it a Christian nation again.

At first, conservative evangelicals turned to the Moral Majority, an organization created by televangelist Jerry Falwell. Utilizing his television show *The Old Time Gospel Hour* as a platform, he sent out a clarion call for Christian conservatives to unite behind his banner.

Falwell proved to be remarkably successful. He was able to enlist hundreds of thousands of supporters for his cause. He probably has good grounds for his claim that he delivered more than eight million votes to Ronald Reagan, thus helping to thwart the reelection bid of Jimmy Carter.

As successful as Falwell proved to be, his influence was to be eclipsed by the campaigning of fellow televangelist Pat Robertson. In 1992, Robertson made a credible attempt to win the Republican nomination for the presidency. He exercised great influence in formulating the party platform and setting the tone of the 1992 National Republican Convention. Robertson was one of the main speakers at the convention, and by taking his place on the podium, he made it abundantly clear that evangelical Christianity was going to be a decisive presence within the Republican Party for years to come.

Perhaps the most important result to come out of Robertson's foray into politics was his joining forces with Ralph Reed. As one of the primary leaders of the Young Republicans (the youth organization of the Republican Party), Reed brought to Robertson all the skills he had learned while working with grassroots political organizations. With Robertson's backing, Reed formed the Christian Coalition, now one of the most powerful political forces in America.

Whereas Falwell and Robertson had previously made their moves on the national political scene, Reed focused on local politics. He organized politically conservative Christians to win elections to local school boards and to run for county and township offices. Reed helped Christians recognize that by securing key offices as committee members in local Republican Parties, they could position themselves to control the destiny of the national party. Within just a couple of years, *USA Today* reported that the Christian Coalition was in control of the Republican Party in eighteen states and was a very strong presence in at least twelve others. As the 1996 presidential race draws near, Reed has been able to serve notice to the Republican Party hierarchy that the concerns of the Christian Coalition are not to be ignored. He has demanded that the Grand Old Party come up with pro-life candidates for both the presidency and the vice presidency, and he has put the "country club Republicans" on notice that his group will not support the party otherwise. Evangelical Christians can no longer be accused of being politically indifferent or unaware of their biblical mandate to change America.

But many evangelicals who had tended toward the political left did not know what to make of all this. They had wanted Christians to be socially active, but they had not counted on them making conservative Republicanism almost synonymous with evangelicalism. All during the 1970s and 1980s, they had joined in the liberal chant of "All power to the people." During the 1990s, they found out who "the people" were.

The politically liberal wing of evangelicalism became concerned that the politics of the Christian Coalition would bring about reversals of legislation they had worked hard to support, legislation that embodied Christian values as *they* understood them. They feared a negation of legislation that had improved the status of women, protected the environment, limited capital punishment, encouraged the upward mobility of people of color, and cut back the militarism of the nation. Evangelicals with politically liberal biases were suddenly concerned that the Christian Coalition was encroaching on the First Amendment rights that guaranteed the separation of church and state. They did not like the results of Christians becoming involved in politics on a massive scale; they began to long for the good old days when the Moral Majority was a silent minority.

Today, some of us have an even deeper concern about something else that is happening as evangelicals become a powerful force in American politics. That is the evidence of a growing *triumphalism* in their rhetoric. More and more, some of us have a concern over calls to "take over the country for Jesus" and to "once again make America a Christian nation." Behind these statements, some of us sense something that hints of totalitarianism. We fear that the goal being sought is to have a nation wherein Christians are able to impose their values and morality on the rest of the populace.

What causes consternation in some ranks is that a number of those who are leading the charge to take over the nation for Christ are committed to a little-known religio-political ideology known as *Reconstructionism.* This philosophy of government, given modern form by Gary North and John Rushdoony, argues that society should be organized in accord with the laws of God as revealed in the Bible. Specifically, the Reconstructionists call for Christians to take over America and enact into law the regulations laid down by Moses in the Pentateuch, the first five books of the Bible.

Upon first encounter, this proposal may not seem so bad, but that is only because most Christians have paid little attention to what is written in the Pentateuch or studied the subtle nuances that scholars discern as they analyze these Mosaic passages. For instance, most of us are unaware of the differences between the "moral laws" of God that are laid down in these books and the "purity codes," also listed in these pages.

For evangelical Christians, the moral laws handed down to Moses abide forever. But for most of us, the purity codes, which also are found in the Pentateuch, were set aside by Jesus and are no longer binding on us. The purity codes are what we would regard as the kosher laws that are observed by extremely orthodox Jews. Jesus Himself refused to observe them in His life here on earth. For instance, Jesus did not observe the regulations concerning touching lepers; nor did He observe all that was involved in Sabbath regulations according to the purity code. He was not about to allow a woman caught in adultery to be stoned to death, even though the purity laws required it.

The book of Acts describes a special revelation given to Peter in a dream in which the purity laws were set aside as God declared clean what the purity code had declared unclean. Following Peter, we evangelical Christians have also set aside the regulations of the purity code. As a case in point, the purity code forbids the wearing of cloth that is woven with mixed fibers. Today Christians feel no guilt about wearing clothing made from a blend of polyester and cotton or any other fibers. When we eat lobster or bacon, we are ignoring the purity code. Yet we do not believe we are condemned by God because we eat these foods. Without even paying much attention to them, we largely ignore the purity law, believing them to belong to a time before Christ established a new freedom for us.

Unfortunately, the Reconstructionists seem to make almost no distinction between the purity laws and the moral laws in the Old Testament. Their rhetoric implies that if they could, they would impose all of the laws of Moses on contemporary society. This is particularly alarming when we realize that the purity laws would require that we stone to death those who commit homosexual acts as well as children who disobey or talk back to their parents. What the Reconstructionists desire for our nation ought to do more than raise our eyebrows!

For me, the problem goes beyond what is sought by those who want to make America into a Christian nation. The real problem is the *means* by which they seek to realize their goal. I do not think that the way to make a society Christian is to gain political power and impose specifically Christian values and rules on the rest of the nation. I believe we are supposed to be at work in this world, trying to change society into the kingdom of God, but I am also convinced that, as the apostle Paul taught us, our weapons or methods are not the methods of this world (2 Cor. 10:4).

I believe that as Christians try to change the world, our means must be through sacrificial love. We are a people who are called to be servants, not masters, and the way we ought to attempt to change things is to use noncoercive methods.

Martin Luther King Jr. changed history through noncoercive means. His crusade for justice was marked by passive resistance against those who would oppress people on the basis of race. Ghandi, likewise, showed us that history can be altered without the use of force. In the end, Ghandi lived out the Sermon on the Mount better than most Christians, and he delivered India from the English, not through violence, but by seeking to overcome evil with good. Neither King nor Ghandi ever held political office; even so, they brought about tremendous change.

Jesus never held political office either, and yet no life in human history has more altered the character of society and the destiny of the kingdoms of this world.

If the Lord had wanted us to set up His kingdom through coercive power, He would have come as a Caesar rather than as a baby in a manger. If He had wanted the power of the stable to be the instrument through which righteousness would be exercised in the nation, He would not have urged His disciples to put away their swords. He would not have warned them, "They that take the sword shall perish with the sword" (Matt. 26:52).

Jesus told Pilate His kingdom was not *of* this world (John 18:36). He certainly did not mean by that statement that His kingdom was not *in* this world. Actually, Jesus made His meaning quite clear when He told His disciples they were to be *in* the world but not *of* it (see John 17:14–18).

What I believe Jesus meant when He said His kingdom was not *of* this world was that it did not come into existence through the means by which kingdoms usually are established—power. Our Lord sought to bring in His kingdom by sacrificially loving people and by meeting their deepest social, psychological, and, most importantly, spiritual needs. He wanted people to respond to Him because they were drawn by His love for them, especially as that love was manifested on the cross: "And I, if I be lifted up from the earth, will draw all men unto me" (John 12:32).

The church that follows the example of Christ will likewise reject coercive power as a means of bringing people into obedience to His will but will instead seek to introduce them to Christ by loving and caring for them in such a way that people will choose to want what Christ wants and to will what Christ wills.

This does not mean we do not vote or hold office. It is just that we must allow people the freedom to live out life as they see fit, as long as their behavior does not violate the rights of others around them. If we all lived like that, our communities would be places of decency and mutual respect. This is not an easy principle to live out in a society as religiously pluralistic as our own. Yet, insofar as it is possible, we must seek to preserve for others the right to live out their convictions, even as we expect them not to flaunt practices or behaviors that will encroach upon what we as a holistic society deem to be the norms of common decency. We should seek to win people to Jesus and the Christian lifestyle rather than coercing them into our way of life. The state rules by coercion, but the church is able to speak to both the state and its citizens with the authority gained through its love and service to others.

As I listen to all of the talk about returning America to being a Christian nation, I have to point out that this nation never *was* as Christian as most advocates of a theocracy seem to think it was. When America was founded, only about 15 percent of the population held membership in any church. Most of the founding fathers, including Franklin, Jefferson, and Washington, were hardly evangelical in their convictions. Jefferson was a Deist and did not believe in the supernatural; Franklin was anything but a faithful churchman. Yet, in their day, the church, though lacking political power, highly influenced the founding of this nation. Out of respect for the church's commitment to the public good, those who wrote the Constitution and the Bill of Rights made certain the principles of Scripture became the basis for our laws. But the church did not establish the spiritual foundations of America by gaining political power and imposing its will on society. Instead, the church acted as the leaven (see Matt. 13:33) and the salt (see Matt. 5:13) and permeated the culture with its values and virtues.

The church in our country's early days was numerically weak, but it was strong in its influence. It was a permeating power, not a dominating force. Today, the church is great numerically; never has there been a time in our history when a greater proportion of our citizens have claimed church membership. Yet in spite of our huge numbers, the influence we have on the current morality of our nation seems to be waning. Could it be that we are losing our influence because, more and more, we are trying to play the political game using Caesar's rules and depending upon power? We seem less and less to be imitating Christ's humility as outlined in the second chapter of Philippians.

Ought we not to be seeking to change the world by emptying ourselves of power and taking on the form of a servant, humbly living out our sacrificial love for the world? It was through a cross that Christ established His Lordship over history. If we are going to follow Him, ought we not to do likewise?

America is a pluralistic society in which there are Jews, Muslims, Buddhists, Hindus, a huge variety of other religions, as well as those who espouse no religion at all. We must not threaten our fellow citizens with a Christian takeover of society nor try to force them to capitulate to our rules. If we take that course, our opportunity to win them to Christ through love will be greatly diminished. Instead, we must work together with others of good will, regardless of their religious traditions, and seek common grounds for morality in order to establish the best society we can build in unity. To do otherwise will put us in danger of the kinds of religious wars that are tearing apart other nations around the world.

A Brief Introduction
to the Next Two Chapters

WHEN WE ASK what Christians ought to do about the poor, we are asking something that is bound to get people upset. There will be those who shrug their shoulders and think they are quoting Scripture when they say, "God helps those who help themselves." These people are not quoting Scripture at all. Instead, they are quoting Benjamin Franklin.

Nevertheless, they have got something important to tell us, and that is that people should assume responsibility for themselves and their own families. They claim that the welfare system in America has been abused by many, and despite whatever good it may have done, it has done a lot of harm. It has destroyed the dignity of many of its recipients and has created what economists call a disincentive to work.

On the other hand, there are those who point out that there are more than nine hundred verses in Scripture reminding Christians that God expects His church to provide for the needs of the poor. But in today's world, poverty is so massive that the church alone cannot do what needs to be done. The financial resources just are not there. Those who work for huge Christian relief organizations like World Vision readily admit that if we are going to alleviate the suffering of poor people around the world we must not only mobilize the church, we must mobilize the resources of government as well.

Is caring for the poor something God expects the church to do apart from government programs? Or should Christians help by supporting the government welfare system? Granted that abuses must be corrected and inefficiencies overcome, can the government's welfare system be viewed as an instrument of God through which His will is done on earth, even as it is in heaven? Is the welfare system a means through which God is able to answer the prayers of the hungry of the world as they pray, "Give us this day our daily bread?"

Answering these questions forces me to divide up this part of the book into two chapters. In the first, I will try to answer questions usually asked about how to determine what the Bible says is the Christian's responsibility to the poor. More specifically, I will endeavor to answer the question asked by many Christians, especially our Roman Catholic brothers and sisters, "Does God have a preference for the poor?"

After giving what I think are biblical answers to these crucial questions, I hope you will then move on with me into the next chapter in which I try to critique some of the ways in which Christians today are trying to respond to the needs of poor people.

I will then briefly explore with you such concerns as whether or not the welfare system in America is something Christians should support. And I hope to help you think through other ways of helping the poor. I will deal extensively with one program in particular that has become quite controversial, the child-support system.

All of this discussion is laden with the kinds of values and principles that are hotly debated, not only in Christian circles, but in society at large. Discussing these issues is something none of us can avoid because in one way or another, our own destinies and the destinies of poor people are wrapped up together. What we decide to do about poor people is crucial to our own being.

15

Does God Prefer Poor People?

WE OFTEN HEAR that God loves all people the same. Speakers at large religious gatherings can usually stir the crowd to shout, "Amen!" by simply stating that, at the foot of the cross, there is a great leveling and that God has no favorites.

All of that sounds great, but increasingly Christians are beginning to ask out loud whether in fact the Lord has a preference for the poor. The pope has said as much (not that his word is binding on evangelical Protestants), and the liberation theologians have endeavored to make the same point. However, the fact that those who are making this claim are viewed by many evangelicals as Marxists is all some evangelicals need to deem the statement to be false.

But before we write off those who make such claims, ought we not first to look at Scripture and see what the Bible has to say about all of this? Consider what Paul said in 1 Corinthians:

> Because the foolishness of God is wiser than men; and the weakness of God is stronger than men.
> For ye see your calling, brethren, how that not many wise men after the flesh, not many mighty, not many noble, are called:

149

But God hath chosen the foolish things of the world
to confound the wise; and God hath chosen the weak
things of the world to confound the things which
are mighty; and base things of the world, and things
which are despised, hath God chosen, yea, and
things which are not, to bring to nought things that
are. (1 Cor. 1:25–28)

From this passage, it seems that God *does* have a preference
for those, the world calls "nothing" and that He chooses them to
be the ones through whom He makes His truth to the world
clearly known.

Some Roman Catholic priests in Latin America have learned
over the past few decades that God uses poor people sacramen-
tally. These priests went into Central and South America with the
expressed purpose of renewing the Catholic Church down there.
They had hopes of bringing Jesus to places where He was not and
of creating spiritual vitality where there was great spiritual leth-
argy. To their surprise, they became the learners rather than the
teachers, the blessed rather than the blessers.

As these missionary priests spread out across Latin America,
they found there was just too much territory for them to cover.
To solve this problem, they came up with a brilliant idea. They
decided to set up "base communities" in villages and towns all
over the Catholic countries to the south of us. In each of them,
people were gathered together and encouraged to do Bible
study. Since a priest was not always at each site, the simple peasants in these base-community Bible studies had to figure out on
their own what the Bible was saying to them.

Those priests in Latin America discovered what church leaders always find when common folks struggle to understand the
Bible with only the Holy Spirit to help them. The peasant villag-
ers came up with some insights into the meaning of Scriptures
that the official clergy had never grasped.

God has a way of revealing His truth to those whom the world
calls "unsophisticated." God imparts great insight to those who
are devoid of the proper "hermeneutics."

Those Catholic priests who had come to Latin America to *bring* the truths of the gospel found that new truths of the gospel were being taught to *them*. What was particularly humbling to these seminary-trained priests and the erudite nuns who accompanied them was that those who were doing the teaching were "ignorant" peasants. Even more humbling for the sophisticated members of the religious intelligentsia, the insights of the peasants had a profundity that could not be denied!

Of all the lessons the Latin American peasants were able to teach the official and ordained priests who had come to preach to them, none was more important than this: "God has sided with the poor and the oppressed against the rich and the powerful." Down through the ages there had always been a struggle between the rich and the poor, between the powerful and the weak, and between the oppressors and the oppressed. But always before there also had been the general conclusion that God was on the side of those who were strong and powerful and rich.

The God about whom the church had always preached was a God who called upon oppressed people to submit to their oppressors without mumbling a word. And the church had Scripture to back up this call to submission. Consider this from the apostle Paul:

> Let every soul be subject unto the higher powers.
> For there is no power but of God: the powers that be
> are ordained of God.
> Whosoever therefore resisteth the power, resisteth
> the ordinance of God: and they that resist shall receive
> to themselves damnation.
> For rulers are not a terror to good works, but to the
> evil. Wilt thou then not be afraid of the power? Do that
> which is good, and thou shalt have praise of the same:
> For he is the minister of God to thee for good. But
> if thou do that which is evil, be afraid; for he beareth
> not the sword in vain: for he is the minister of God, a
> revenger to execute wrath upon him that doeth evil.
> (Rom. 13:1–4)

Following through on this biblical admonition, the Catholic Church in Latin America had always concluded that those who held the reins of power, wealth, and prestige had been ordained for their roles by the Almighty. So when the dictators of Latin American countries stood on their balconies to wave at the crowds, almost always the archbishop of the church would stand beside them. The presence of a prince of the church gave essential legitimation to the power and authority of the dictator. In the eyes of everyone on the scene, there could be no doubt as to where God had taken His stand. From Samosa, the iron-fisted dictator who ruled Nicaragua from 1936 until 1956, to Batista, who established a cruel and corrupt police state in Cuba in the 1930s, the message was the same: God had sided with the rich and the powerful against the poor and the oppressed. The poor and the oppressed seemed to be called by God to "be subject unto the higher powers."

Now, all of a sudden, groups of peasants in base communities were questioning this conventional religious wisdom and calling for a reversal of things. They were giving what seemed to be a topsy-turvy interpretation of what God was doing in history. In these base communities, common people were articulating the incredible message that the official church had gotten it all wrong, that instead of siding with the rich and the powerful, God had sided with the poor and the oppressed.

What is more, these peasants were saying they had the Bible to prove it. They pointed out that in the Old Testament, out of all the nations of the earth, God had chosen an impoverished, enslaved people to be His elect nation. As the people of Israel cried out in their sufferings, Yahweh had heard their cries and promised to fight for them and to deliver them from the hands of their oppressors.

What could it mean when God chose a downtrodden group of Jews to be His special instrument of blessing to all the rest of the people in the world? The peasants said it meant the God of the Bible preferred a poor, beaten, and enslaved people to the rich and the powerful.

When the people of Israel eventually got to the promised land, it did not take long before social classes emerged. As sociologists commonly observe even today, wealth tends to become concentrated in the hands of a few while the masses become increasingly poor. It is something sociologists call the "iron law of oligarchy." There is always a small group of people who make it their primary concern to gather this world's goods and who do it better than the rest of us. When these people acquire wealth, they seem easily to translate it into political power, which in turn enables them to protect their economic interests.

What makes this process evil is that in protecting their own interests, members of the wealthy ruling class usually ignore the welfare of others. When the rich gain power, they generally use it in a way that leads to the oppression of the poor. It is then that God moves against them.

That is what happened in the days of the Hebrew prophets. Those in Israel who were rich lived lives of luxury at the expense of the poor. The rich enjoyed their "good life," and they did so with an air of indifference to the plight of those who did not have even the basic necessities of life.

All of the Old Testament prophets railed against the wealthy ones who demonstrated such irresponsibility toward the poor around them. The major thrust of their prophetic message was a condemnation of the hardhearted rich. The prophet Amos cried out:

> [The rich] lie upon beds of ivory, and stretch themselves upon their couches, and eat the lambs out of the flock, and the calves out of the midst of the stall. . . .
> Therefore now shall they go captive with the first that go captive, and the banquet of them that stretched themselves shall be removed. (Amos 6:4, 7)

And no less severe with his message was the prophet Isaiah, who said:

> Woe unto them that decree unrighteous decrees, and that write grievousness which they have prescribed;

To turn aside the needy from judgment, and to take away the right from the poor of my people, that widows may be their prey, and that they may rob the fatherless!

And what will ye do in the day of visitation, and in the desolation which shall come from far? To whom will you flee for help? And where will ye leave your glory? (Isa. 10:1–3)

The writings of the Old Testament prophets leave no room for doubt. God has sided with the poor and the oppressed, and He champions their cause against the rich and the powerful.

When we come to the New Testament, the message seems to be the same. The Virgin Mary in her great hymn of praise following the Annunciation declared:

For he that is mighty hath done to me great things; and holy is his name.

And his mercy is on them that fear him from generation to generation.

He hath shewed strength with his arm; he hath scattered the proud in the imagination of their hearts.

He hath put down the mighty from their seats, and exalted them of low degree.

He hath filled the hungry with good things; and the rich He hath sent empty away. (Luke 1:49–53)

Such a proclamation leaves no doubt that Mary's son is to be the deliverer of the poor and will bring down the wealthy elite.

When Jesus initiated His ministry some thirty years later, He made it clear that His gospel was good news for the poor and deliverance for the oppressed captives of the world (see Luke 4:18). And all through Jesus' ministry, He made it clear that it is the poor who are the most blessed in His eyes. He said this clearly in the Beatitudes, as given in Luke 6:20–21:

And he lifted up his eyes on his disciples, and said, Blessed be ye poor: for yours is the kingdom of God.

> Blessed are ye that hunger now: for ye shall be filled.
> Blessed are ye that weep now: for ye shall laugh.

Jesus' message about His preference for the poor remained consistent throughout His ministry. When a rich young ruler came to Him asking for eternal life, Jesus told him to sell all he had and give it to the poor.

Needless to say, such admonitions to rich people troubled Jesus' followers back then even as they disturb Christians in today's world. They wondered, even as we do now, whether Jesus was saying that rich people are going to be excluded from the kingdom of God. The answer Jesus gave to that inquiry scares all of us who have more than enough of this world's wealth. Jesus said: "It is easier for a camel to go through the eye of a needle, than for a rich man to enter into the kingdom of God" (Mark 10:25).

The ultimate statement about how Jesus regards poor people is shown in what He said about judgment day. In the well-known passage, Matthew 25:31–46, He said that on that great day, we will be judged on the basis of how we responded to the sufferings of the hungry, naked, sick, imprisoned, and alien peoples among us. Jesus let it be known that He is a spiritual presence in the poor. For us in our time, Jesus chooses to present Himself through the poor and the oppressed, and He lets it be known that there *is* a special preference on His part to be loved in them.

But it does not end there. In the Epistles of the New Testament, this same preference for the poor is cited over and over again. Nowhere in the Epistles is this more clear than in the writings of James. Those passages give us some idea as to how very much our God prefers poor people over rich people.

> Hearken, my beloved brethren, hath not God chosen
> the poor of this world rich in faith, and heirs of the
> kingdom which he hath promised to them that love him?

But ye have despised the poor. Do not rich men oppress you, and draw you before the judgment seats? (James 2:5–6)

And later on in this little epistle, James let it be known that being rich is not a desirable state for a Christian:

Go to now, ye rich men, weep and howl for your miseries that shall come upon you.

Your riches are corrupted, and your garments are motheaten.

Your gold and silver is cankered; and the rust of them shall be a witness against you, and shall eat your flesh as it were fire. Ye have heaped treasure together for the last days. (James 5:1–3)

You cannot read such passages without getting the sense that the gospel may be good news for the poor, but it sounds like bad news for the rich.

What are we to make of all of this? Are we to feel guilty because of our wealth? Should we give away everything we have, as the Bible apparently directs us to do? Are we all supposed to live like the Franciscan monks of the Middle Ages? And most important, what is supposed to be the response of people as rich as we are to the needs of the poor?

Certainly our response to the poor is meant to be more than a good motivational talk and a word of prayer. In words dripping with sarcasm, the apostle James said that more than that is expected of us.

What doth it profit, my brethren, though a man say he hath faith, and have not works? Can faith save him?

If a brother or sister be naked, and destitute of daily food, and one of you say unto them, "Depart in peace, be ye warmed and filled"; notwithstanding ye give them not those things which are needful to the body; what doth it profit? (James 2:14–16)

The apostle John made an even more specific judgment of those who fail to respond to the needs of the poor. He wrote, "Little children, let no man deceive you: he that doeth righteousness is righteous, even as he is righteous" (1 John 3:7).

But just how are we to do righteousness? How are we to go about giving to the poor in a way that will really help them? How do we keep from creating lazy people who live in a state of dependency? How do we keep those who constantly ask for a handout from losing their dignity? And how do we prevent those to whom we give from ending up resentful toward the very people who sacrificed to meet their needs? Finally, how do we translate our Christian responsibility to help the poor into social policy for ours, the richest nation on the earth? In the next chapter I'll attempt to offer some solutions for these perplexing and challenging questions.

16

What Should Christians Do about the Welfare System?

WHEN WE TALK to rich Christians, it is best to explain that it is no sin to make a lot of money, but it may be a sin to keep it. John said people must question whether they are really Christians at all if they hold on to their wealth while they see others around them in desperate need.

I remember well being in Haiti with my son Bart when he was a little boy. We were walking down the main street of Port-au-Prince when a ragged and dirty child confronted us, pathetically holding out his cupped hands to beg some pennies from us. "Bart!" I said. "Don't give him anything! If you give him so much as a nickel, every poor kid in Port-au-Prince will be on us in no time, and they won't let us alone until they've got every cent we have."

"So?" was my son's answer, unforgettable and piercing to my heart.

What an obvious response for a Christian: "So?" What Bart was saying to me in that monosyllable was that when you have money, you ought to be ready to surrender it to poor and desperate people (see Matt. 5:42).

In Haiti, when confronted by starving children, it seems pretty obvious what we should do. But what about on the streets of New York when you are confronted by a derelict who looks like he's freaked out on drugs? Are we not hurting a man like that if we give him money he will probably use to nurse a crack addiction? Would it not be more Christian simply to pass him by?

One of my friends has tried to address such a problem by going to McDonald's and buying several booklets of gift certificates. Each of the certificates can be traded in for a basic meal. So whenever anyone begs for some money to buy food he gives him or her a McDonald's gift certificate. My friend knows it is not a perfect solution to the problem, but it seems better to him, and to me, than giving out money in such circumstances.

My wife and I were at an underground station in London when we were approached by a woman who asked me for some money. She said she needed the money to buy food for the child she was holding in her arms.

An English woman walking behind us called out to me, "Don't give her anything! She'll only use it on booze." I thought for just a moment, and this simple truth seemed clear: Giving to that woman was my responsibility. What she did with the money after I gave it to her was her responsibility.

God puts the wealth in our hands without any guarantees from us that we will use what He gives us in a way that pleases Him. He trusts us. Ought we not to do to others what He has done for us?

On that great day when I stand before Him, He will ask if I gave to the needy. I do not think it will wash if I say, "I thought about it, but they did not look trustworthy."

The Lord just might answer such an excuse by saying, "You should have done what I asked you to do. In turn, I would have held them responsible for what they did with the money."

On the societal level, the problem becomes more complex. More than a half-century ago, the U.S. government initiated a welfare system. It was supposed to be a safety net for those who fell on bad times or had difficulties that prevented them from supporting themselves. During the years of President Lyndon B. Johnson, this basic welfare system was expanded into what came to be called the "Great Society" programs.

Sadly, what began as our honest and compassionate attempt to help the poor has turned into a nightmare of abuse and waste. Charles Murray, a politically conservative economist, outlined the impact of the Great Society programs in his book *Losing Ground*. With well-documented statistics, Murray makes his case that the welfare programs of the Great Society years only made things worse. Benefits offered by the welfare system were so generous that they discouraged people from getting jobs. For instance, according to one estimate, a person in the Los Angeles area would have to earn $7.50 an hour just to *equal* the benefits that welfare agencies would provide her or him in grants, food stamps, and services. Murray argues that for many people, the welfare system has destroyed all incentive to work.

Over the course of three decades, welfare has become a way of life for millions of Americans. There are huge numbers of able-bodied men and women who have shirked their responsibility to earn a living and learned to live off the labors of others.

There is nothing new about such people. They were around in the days of the early church. And Paul had some harsh words for them: "For even when we were with you, this we commanded you, that if any would not work, neither should he eat" (2 Thess. 3:10).

You don't have to be a right-wing Republican to be horrified at what has happened to the welfare system in America. Even liberal Democrats are appalled by the situation. There are calls from all quarters to carry out wide-ranging reforms on the welfare system. There may be conflicting views about what should be done, and there may be a lot of political games being played, but one thing is certain: The long-term free ride for able-bodied persons is over. All parties in Washington are agreed that, for people who are able to work, the time limit for receiving welfare will be two years.

All of this sounds good, except for the fact that there are many able-bodied men and women who are not employable. There are some minimum-wage jobs available, but a minimum-wage job without benefits does not enable a person to support a family. The fact is that there simply are not enough jobs that pay decent wages for all of those who could work and are now on the welfare rolls.

William Julius Wilson, a University of Chicago sociologist, argues convincingly in his book *The Truly Disadvantaged* that hundreds of thousands of able-bodied men and women are on welfare because of what he calls the deindustrialization of America. Over the past quarter of a century, Wilson says, either because of automation or the exporting of heavy industries to Third World countries, America has lost huge numbers of high-paying jobs that were once available to semi-skilled laborers.

It is all good and well to call for those who formerly worked in these industries to be retrained to do the more skilled work that goes with our computerized economy, but it is just not that easy. Many of those on welfare, for one reason or another, do not fit into these retraining schemes. Computers threaten some people, and others are just too far behind to gain the kind of education that would make them viable in the new technology of the marketplace.

Those of us in the church cannot help but ask whether we have a responsibility to do something about all this. Is it the responsibility of the church to create decent-paying jobs for men and women who seem to be left out of the new economics of America and who are about to be thrown off the welfare rolls?

When there were no hospitals, the church created hospitals. When there were no schools, the church created schools. And when there were no recreational facilities, the church created the YMCAs and the YWCAs. Now people, especially poorly educated people, are crying out for jobs. Shouldn't the church create those necessary jobs? Isn't job creation the best alternative to welfare?

Consider the fact that most churches have all that is necessary to serve as an incubator for a micro-business. First of all, there is the building the church owns. In the majority of instances, most of the building space remains unused from Sunday to Sunday. Couldn't the church building be used during the week to house entrepreneurial enterprises sponsored by the church? Such use would not necessarily preclude the use of the same rooms for church school on Sundays.

Churches usually have offices fully equipped with typewriters, word processors, duplicating machines, and the other office equipment so essential for most business ventures. The church secretary or volunteers from the congregation could help out with the office work for these new companies in their early stages of development.

In most of the old, established churches, especially in the inner city where these new entrepreneurial enterprises are most needed, there are retired members who have experience in business and industry. Couldn't these church members serve as consultants to new enterprises being started up by the church?

There are almost unlimited ideas as to what businesses and micro-industries could be started. Here are just a few:

- Recharging cartridges for word processors and laser printers
- Rebuilding alternators and generators for automobiles
- Silk-screen printing of posters, T-shirts, and greeting cards
- Production of nails and other hardware items
- Production of fish flies
- A moving business (Trucks can be rented as needed.)
- A cleaning business

It is possible for a church in a needy community to create scores of jobs and thus help relatively unskilled laborers become business partners. Is this not a better way for Christians to respond to the needs of the poor than welfare?

There is something more to be said about the welfare system and how the church can respond to it. Would it not be possible to establish a system in which the church and the state cooperate with each other to help the poor? Surely there is a way for this to be done without violating the principle of separation of church and state.

Consider the possibility of the government entering into partnership with churches as well as with synagogues, mosques, and other voluntary community organizations. These independent institutions would agree to provide special care for specific welfare families. A given church or other voluntary organization might assume responsibility for five or six needy families. Instead of money being handed out to them, each family would be given a variety of vouchers to be exchanged for food, rent, day-care services, medical care, and other necessities. The church could assume responsibility for ensuring the proper use of these vouchers. Through such a cooperative arrangement, the probability of the abuse of welfare benefits would be dramatically lessened.

Perhaps the best reason to bring private institutions such as churches into cooperation with the government to help solve the welfare problems of America is that the people in organizations like the church have connections. The associations church members have with people in the larger community would provide a viable network to help unemployed people find jobs. Such a network would probably beat anything presently being provided at the employment agencies run by the state.

There is another kind of welfare we cannot overlook or neglect. That is our gifts to help meet the needs of people in Third World countries.

These days, there is more and more evidence that Americans want to withdraw from the responsibilities that go with being the richest country in the world. Increasingly, Americans feel that too many of our tax dollars are being given away to poor countries overseas and that the time has come to cut back.

In response to such talk, I have to say, first of all, that we really aren't giving away as much as people think. Out of each tax dollar we send to Washington, only five cents is given away to poor people *both at home and abroad.* We like to think of ourselves as the most generous people on earth, but on a per capita basis we are ranked way below countries such as Japan, Denmark, Norway, Sweden, and Germany. Actually we are seventeenth on the list of giving nations in terms of per capita giving. We seem to forget the words of Jesus, who told us that to whom much is given, much is required (see Luke 12:48).

I was appalled to hear some U.S. senators who are well-known Christians call for a cut in aid to Third World countries. In the case of Haiti, they said we had no business sending our troops there to restore democracy and establish order since "Haiti serves none of our national interests."

These senators seem to forget that the poverty and oppression of Haiti is largely the consequence of a family of dictators we supported and financed for almost half a century. We undergirded tyrants for no other reason than that they served our interests in establishing noncommunist regimes close to our shores. The suffering of the Haitian people was ignored until, in desperation, they began forming armadas of small boats that brought them to Florida. It was then that our government decided to send in the marines.

The situation in Haiti presents us with an excellent opportunity to use our foreign aid to do some nation building. And we should do it even though Haiti doesn't have oil as Kuwait does. We should send in the army engineers to help rebuild the roads, bridges, electric-generating plants, and other necessities for an industrial subculture so the needy people of this suffering country can develop a job-creating economy. We must send in our experts in agriculture and provide Haiti with the help needed to rebuild the land that has been all but destroyed by deforestation and erosion. We ought to do all these things because it is right and also because God blesses people in order that they might be a blessing to others.

Even when it comes to helping the poor in Third World countries, we need to consider forging some alliances between the government and the church. Together we can do incredible things.

In Canada, the government (which incidentally is radically separated from the church) has found it extremely advantageous to cooperate with the church when it comes to helping people in poor countries. The Canadians have found that missionary organizations and other "voluntary organizations" are able to deliver services to poor people much more cost-efficiently than can government bureaucracies. This effectiveness is so evident that those involved have worked out a program in which the government will match dollar for dollar what the church gives for a social program such as the development of a school or an agricultural project. This alliance has resulted in some brilliant successes in foreign aid with minimal investments by the government.

The United States has picked up on this idea and developed some special arrangements with what is called private voluntary organizations, or PVOs. In each case, the PVO operates social services and economic development projects that do not directly involve the proclamation of the gospel.

For instance, World Vision, the world's largest Christian relief organization, really is two separate organizations. Through one organization that is closely connected to evangelistic efforts, it does ministry directly related to indigenous churches in Third World countries. The other World Vision organization, which uses government grants to carry out development work in poor nations, develops and maintains programs that are not tied in *directly* with the proclamation of the gospel. Of course, whenever the poor are served and the hungry are fed, we see the signs of the kingdom of God. But by operating as two organizations,

World Vision carefully observes the separation of church and state and thus makes it possible for church people to do the work of God in cooperation with the state in a way that fits the requisites of the Constitution.

This cooperative scheme, which separates World Vision's economic and social development programs from the preaching of the gospel, allows Christian people to help the government accomplish much for the poor in a most efficient and cost-effective way. Jesus must be pleased with such an arrangement.

We cannot walk away from the poor. We must respond to their needs. God prefers to be among them, and if we want to be close to God, we must be among them too.

As we look for ways to respond to the poor, we must never be so overwhelmed by what seems impossible that we shy away from that which we could do. Mother Teresa once said, "If you cannot feed a hundred, then feed one." Whatever you think about my ideas on welfare and foreign aid, please give some consideration to doing something for at least one little kid who even now languishes in some poor village or urban slum in the Third World. For just twenty-four dollars a month (that's eighty-five cents a day—less than you pay for a cup of coffee), you can provide a needy child with the basic support for a decent life. For just eighty-five cents a day, you can make it possible for that child to be housed, clothed, fed, educated, and most important of all, evangelized.

Questions may be raised by skeptics who wonder whether the money really gets where it's supposed to go. Well, I cannot vouch for all the organizations that have child-support programs, but I can vouch for the one I think is best: Compassion International. Both my son and I have gone to the field and worked with the people of Compassion International firsthand. There are other organizations that claim to be able to support a child for less than Compassion International does, but most of them do not provide the kind of supervision over how each dollar is spent that the Compassion people do.

Compassion keeps track of every child, and that is not an easy task. Among the poor in Third World countries, children are often moved around from place to place. One week the child is living with one family and the next week with another. Keeping track of the whereabouts of the children is a problem, even as it is a problem to ensure that the money provided for the care of the child is properly spent. The extra few dollars it costs to support a child with Compassion International is an investment that makes possible the wise and careful use of the money given. Many of the other programs cannot match this kind of carefulness.

There are those who raise the question as to whether or not the whole child-support system is a mistake. I heard of one situation in which money was provided for some of the children of a village to go to school and to get properly fed, but there was not enough for all the children of that village. The end result was that some children in the village had their needs met, but other children could only look on and longingly watch.

Such a thing would not happen in a village where Compassion works. Compassion people work hard to see that resources are shared and that no one nearby is left out. Often what is provided for one child is shared by others in the same family. Great effort is expended to see that no child eats while another watches in hunger. The Compassion programs are more comprehensive in their scope than those kinds of child-support programs that would permit such inequity.

If you choose to support a child through an organization other than Compassion International, you need to ask questions to be sure you are not contributing to any abusive practices like the one I have just described.

Another objection that is often raised about child-support programs is that the money would better be spent on economic and community-development programs such as those sponsored by groups like World Concern, based in Seattle, Washington. Indeed, development programs are what ultimately help the poor in Third World countries to help themselves. But as crucial as development programs are, they do not rescue the kids whose immediate needs are going unmet.

It is all well and good to put money into agricultural programs and fish farms that will provide food for an entire poor community in a Third World country. But between now and the time the objectives of such projects are realized, we cannot let individual kids go hungry. Between now and the time when we develop ways of rescuing the many, we must provide for ways to meet the immediate needs of as many individual kids as possible.

Child-support programs are not the ultimate answer to the needs of people in Third World countries, but they are wonderful, temporary instruments of deliverance for a lot of children who would otherwise get lost and even die.

Why not support a child through Compassion International? Write to:

COMPASSION INTERNATIONAL
3955 Cragwood Drive
Box 7000
Colorado Springs, Colorado 80933

They will sign you up with a specific child, send you a photo of that child, and make sure you get regular letters from him or her.

On that great day of judgment, when the Lord (who has a preference for the poor) asks you what *you* did for Him in your earthly sojourn, it would be a good thing to have a child speak up for you and say, "I don't know what she did for You, Lord, but I was hungry and she fed me. I was naked and she bought clothes for me. I couldn't afford to go to school and she made it possible for me to get an education. I was sick and she paid for a doctor. And most important, Lord, I did not know who You were, and she made it possible for me to hear the good news about You and Your kingdom."

Then the Lord will say to you, "Enter into My kingdom. Because what you did for that child, you did for Me."

Conclusion

Should Christians
Avoid Controversy?

I KNOW THAT a book like this will get me into a lot of trouble. There will be those who are offended by some of the things I have written. I would like them to know I had no desire to upset them.

There will be others who argue that I am off the mark in my use of Scripture and that I have misinterpreted some of the passages that play a heavy role in what I have to say. I would like them to know I tried very hard to remain faithful to the biblical message and to interpret Scripture within the parameters of orthodox evangelical Christianity.

There will be those who say that what I have written is not in line with what they believe to be at the heart of conservative evangelical Christianity. But I *am* an evangelical Christian! I believe in the doctrines of the Apostles' Creed, and I believe the Bible is an infallible revelation from God given under the inspiration of the Holy Spirit. If I do not seem to fit the mold of conservative evangelicalism, perhaps it is because I try not to be "knee-jerk" in my reactions when issues are raised. On some issues, such as whether we should have sex education in public schools, I will come across as an *extreme* conservative. On other issues, such as whether gay men and lesbian women should have the same rights as other people, I will come across as a liberal. Furthermore, I urge other Christians to take this same approach in dealing with the issues we have to face in our complex world. Consider each issue separately.

I believe Christians should not simply align themselves with a given sociopolitical stance and then make all their decisions on the basis of what will fit into an already-established mind-set. Instead, we need to bring to each and every social concern and ethical issue a deep commitment to finding out what the Bible has to say about the topic at hand. Through prayer, reflection, and study, each of us is called upon to work out his or her own salvation with fear and trembling (see Phil. 2:12).

We need a new kind of politics in America that will refuse to buy into the party labels of the past. There are those who would make Christianity synonymous with the agenda of the liberal policies of the Democratic Party. On the other hand, many evangelicals think the Christian Coalition and the right wing of the Republican Party is the best expression of God's will for America. In reality, if we are to be truly Christian, we must transcend such doctrinaire ideological approaches to the issues of our day. We must learn to think through things, just as Paul admonished the Philippian church: "Let this mind be in you, which was also in Christ Jesus" (Phil. 2:5).

The problem with partisan politics is that each party strives to serve the interests of its own specific constituency. Historically, the Democratic Party has tended to serve the interests of labor unions, people of color, and socially disinherited people such as homosexuals and aliens. On the other hand, the Republican Party has tended to represent the interests of the broad middle class of this country as well as the interests of corporate America. God transcends such limited interests and seeks for His people to do justice for all.

As I wrote this book, there were those who told me I was giving a lot of ammunition to my enemies. One of my friends said,

"If you don't want people to shoot at you, why do you give them so many bullets to put in their guns?"

The truth is that people who want to "get" me will get me, no matter what I say or do. My experience has been that even when I play it safe and say all of the "right" things, those who want to shoot me down find a way to do it anyway. They twist what I say and manage to make it sound like the opposite of what I meant. If that does not work, they make up things. There are people who think they are true defenders of the faith because they work hard to detect in others anything that might have implications that could possibly sound like heresy. When a person comes with such a witch-hunting attitude, there is not a thing anybody can do to straighten things out.

But there is something else to be considered. If we confine ourselves to saying only what is safe, we will find ourselves incapable of saying much that is significant. If we are going to speak out on the difficult issues of our times, we must be ready to take risks, because the answers to the tough questions are seldom clear-cut. Those who dare to address the controversial and diverse issues that challenge us must first consider how Scripture is related to the concern at hand. Then, after spending time reading, thinking, and praying, it is time to wait on the Lord for both the directive and the courage to speak out.

Very often, after I have addressed some controversial issue and expressed what I believe to be a biblical perspective on it, some evangelical leaders will tell me they are glad I said what I did. They often follow up by saying they feel and think the same way I do but they are in no position to speak out on the subject. When I ask them why they are so reluctant to step out and let their views be known, they almost always answer, "I *have* to think about the effect it would have on my ministry."

In most instances, what they really mean is that they need to raise a lot of money either to sustain the staff members and the organizational structures that keep some very worthwhile mission work in place, or they have to support their own television and radio ministries. It takes a solid financial base and a good cash flow to keep such things going. For most evangelical organizations, the alleviation of even a small proportion of supporters could prove disastrous. The maintenance of the ministry and the efforts of its leadership to do the good things they believe God has called them to do could be jeopardized by a leader who "speaks out."

I fully understand this kind of thinking. I have helped establish an array of missionary programs over the years. They are all very precious to me, and much of my life and my own financial resources have been invested in them. If they go under, I will be heartbroken. Yet I know that if I take definitive positions on controversial issues, I will alienate some of the givers who make these ministries possible.

All of this generates a certain reluctance on my part to say what I really think and believe on the hard issues and difficult problems of our times. I am surely tempted to play it safe for the sake of the missionary work I believe God has given me to do.

My concerns about maintaining a financial base for the missionary work that I support weigh heavily upon me. One of our ministries has work in Haiti. Should I risk alienating supporters who help me feed and educate large numbers of Haitian children? Here in the United States I have helped establish a variety of programs that provide the only real chance for a positive future for hundreds of inner-city kids. Do I really have the right to speak out on controversial issues when what I say could diminish the essential financial support that keeps these ministries alive and well?

As I ask such questions of myself, I know that others far more prominent than I are asking themselves the same questions. The televangelist who needs $250,000 a week to keep his programs on the air is asking how his ability to get the gospel out to millions of listeners and watchers will be affected if any of his supporters are angered by something he says.

The Christian psychologist who does so much good through

counseling people daily on his or her radio show has to ask whether a true expression of his or her beliefs about the causes of homosexuality might result in a drop in the giving that buys air time. Such are the concerns of all prominent spokespersons for the Christian faith. Ministry costs a lot of money these days, and it is easy to conclude that preserving one's ministry should take precedence over all else.

I struggled with all of this as I put together this book, and I want to share with you the conclusion I have reached. I have come to believe that all of "my" ministries and missionary work are not really mine at all. They belong to the Lord. Furthermore, maintaining them is His problem, not mine. As I have decided to speak out on the issues that haunt this generation, I have also concluded that God has not so much asked me to be successful in my ministries as He has asked me to be faithful to my convictions and to those concerns He has laid on my heart. That is why I have decided to speak out and to take the risks that go with being outspoken and straightforward.

For too long, Christian leaders have been unwilling to take risks that go with the prophetic ministry Christ has given to His church. Too often, religious leaders play games with His church and its people and speak ambiguously, as politicians often do, so as not to endanger their ministries. Caution may be a virtue, but cowardice certainly isn't anything to write home to Mother about.

Too many of us in Christian ministry are more concerned about leaving a legacy than in being faithful. Far too many of us are more concerned about leaving something behind that bears our name than we are about saying what we think is right or wrong about the hot issues of our times. We all know there are "hot buttons" that need to be pushed, and yet we are afraid to push them. We evade the controversial issues that confront us and profess that we are still being faithful because we have preserved *our* ministries.

James the Apostle said when you speak you should "let your yea be yea; and your nay, nay" (James 5:12). What he was urging us to do is speak with straightforwardness and clarity when we talk to those around us. Hedging and evading are not what Christians should be about as they converse either with each other or with the world outside.

There is no excuse for the ambiguities that often mark our public utterances. In too many cases, after a religious leader addresses a controversial issue, I wonder what he or she has said. The words are so obtuse and the meaning is so vague that when all is said and done, *nothing* has been said or done.

I have tried to speak to the issues targeted in this book in such a way that you, the reader, will know exactly where I stand; I am fully aware of the consequences of being honest. The alternative is to be unfaithful to what the Lord expects of us all.

So I take my chances with you. I do so with a fearfulness that what I say from my heart could hurt certain ministries I have spent a lifetime building up. I am trusting God to give me the courage to overcome these fears.

What must go along with stepping out and trying to define Christian postures on controversial subjects is a willingness to be corrected. No one is more aware than I am that I could be wrong. None of us knows for sure that what we are saying is free from distortion.

In the end, the only thing I have certainty about is that Jesus is Lord, Savior, and God, and that the Bible is an inerrant record of what God has done and is doing for us. Like the apostle Paul, I can only be sure of what I am talking about when I preach Christ, and Him crucified (see 1 Cor. 2:2).

If we are going to maintain a cutting edge in what we speak and write, we have to run the risk of being misunderstood and of making mistakes. This is all a part of what goes with entering into the marketplace of ideas and being a part of the ongoing discussions that go with that in both the Christian community and the secular society.

If we are going to *have* Christian intellectuals, we must offer them graciousness when they make errors. We must be ready to correct them in love. Certainly, we must resist the temptation to jump all over them when we disagree with them or to run them out of the Christian community because their ideas do not neatly fit in with our assumptions of what Christianity is all about.

If we are not allowed to make mistakes, we will never dare to say the things that have to be said or address any of our real contemporary problems. On the other hand, if we are not ready to hear criticisms and, when necessary, correct ourselves, we set in motion trends that can do much damage to the church.

Let it be known that I am ready to be corrected. I take criticism of what I say and write very seriously. Do not think that any letter you write to me will be tossed in the wastebasket. I will read what you say and give it careful consideration. I learn much from my critics, especially from those who speak the truth in love (see Eph. 4:15).

Karl Barth, the controversial German-Swiss theologian, once said that each of us should start every day by reading the Bible, which we hold in one hand, and the newspaper, which we hold in the other. That is what I have tried to do in putting together this book.

Should you want to write and let me know what you think, my address is:

EASTERN COLLEGE
10 Fairview Drive
St. Davids, Pennsylvania 19087

Some of you may want to support the missionary work to which I have committed my life. Let me tell you a little bit about it. The Evangelical Association for the Promotion of Education (EAPE) has attempted to capitalize on the idealistic and altruistic impulses of young people and channel them into service for the poor and the oppressed. Each year more than three hundred young people work with us both overseas in Haiti and in the urban ghettos of our own country.

In Haiti our workers have come up with an incredibly original and cost-effective plan. In more than fifty villages of that poverty-stricken and politically oppressed nation, they have established what we call literacy centers. In setting up these centers, we have abandoned the American concept of education. Instead of taking kids from kindergarten through twelfth grade, we offer special programs that, over a two-year period, teach children (and adults) only how to read and write and do arithmetic. We are a Christian ministry and provide this basic education in the name of Jesus Christ.

Each of these literary centers is a small school with somewhere between ten and thirty students. We have found that when we get the children at about ten or eleven years of age, we can teach them to read and write in a very short period of time.

Some of our literacy centers concentrate on adult education. When working with adults, we find that literacy can be achieved in less than a year. Adults can also learn basic mathematics in that time.

The cost of running each of these literacy centers is phenomenally low; each of them costs only eighteen hundred dollars per year. We are able to keep the cost down because we use Haitians as teachers. Our EAPE staff people coordinate their work and are responsible for training teachers.

Here in the United States, our programs are varied. During the summer we have almost 250 collegians who work with us without any pay at all. They give us their entire summer to work among children and teenagers located in eighteen different neighborhoods in the urban slums of this country.

From 9:00 in the morning until 1:00 in the afternoon, they work with children in day-camp programs, doing the things you might expect in a camp: arts and crafts, sports, cultural-enrichment programs, music programs, and most important for us, a great deal of Bible study.

The evenings are set aside to work with teenagers. We have club programs for almost every interest, as well as sports programs, and we have a strong focus on evangelism. We believe that unless these high school kids have a spiritual awakening, they have little hope for the future. We urge our workers to spend the afternoons (if they have any energy left) doing one-on-one relational ministry. They take individual children to museums, on picnics, to the zoo, etc. It is the one-on-one interaction with these children that brings about the most effective changes. Children respond to personalized, loving concern.

During the regular school year, we run after-school programs. We are incredibly ecumenical and use any church buildings available for our program. At each site, we try to integrate the children into the life of those respective churches. The after-school programs are not only recreational; they have a strong emphasis on tutoring. Our commitment is to help the thousands of children whose lives we touch to know Jesus Christ and to become successful citizens.

We also run evening programs for teenagers. These year-round programs are maintained by young people we call interns. Following graduation from college, these committed short-term missionaries give us a year or two of their lives before going on with their own vocational plans. I have to say, however, that after working with inner-city kids, a good number of these interns choose to give the rest of their lives to working with the poor and the oppressed.

EAPE has also established Cornerstone Christian Academy, a special school in Philadelphia. It serves African-American children and is focused on the most socially disadvantaged children of the city. We concentrate on drawing youngsters from the government housing projects.

Our classes never have more than twenty students. There is a teacher and a teacher's aide in each class, and in all we do, there is a great spiritual emphasis. We feel that the latter is responsible for creating the new self-image that is necessary to keep these kids from viewing themselves as losers.

Our latest effort has been in economic development. Working

with the Philadelphia Development Partnership, we have initiated a number of businesses and industries that young people can start and own themselves. We've started a T-shirt factory and have experimented with a few other industries, creating employment for scores of teenagers who previously just hung out on the corners. We really believe that job creation in the ghetto is crucial to the success of working with young people. Of all the social needs that inner-city youth have, jobs are at the top of the list. Where none exist, we feel we must do our best to create them.

Finally, we are making a strong effort to train inner-city young people to be leaders in their own churches and communities. Through weekend conferences, summer training programs, and special seminars, we are raising up a new generation of African-American and Hispanic leaders. We believe that in them lies our best hope for the social and spiritual development of urban America.

If you want to support these ministries, make out your check to the Evangelical Association for the Promotion of Education and send it to:

EAPE
Box 7238
St. Davids, Pennsylvania 19087–7238

Unless you indicate otherwise, I will then add your name and address to our mailing list so you can receive our monthly newsletter.

Thanks for reading this book! And thanks for being willing to think along with me.

Sincerely,
Tony Campolo

P. S.

STARTING IN October 1995, the prominent preacher Steve Brown from Orlando, Florida, will be joining me to do a weekly television show on the Vision/Acts cable network. Watch for our shows, because they will be a television extension of this book. Steve and I will go back and forth on many of the topics I have handled in this book. Together we will try to model the ways that Christians can disagree, learn from each other, and use the Bible in working through the hot issues of our society.

A book like this one can be used for adult Sunday school classes because it provides "take-off" places for intense discussion. You might also consider taping our television show and playing it to your Sunday school class. This is still another way to get discussions going on the issues that challenge us as Christians.

OTHER BOOKS BY TONY CAMPOLO

A Reasonable Faith
Carpe Diem
How to Be Pentecostal Without Speaking in Tongues
It's Friday but Sunday's Comin'
Partly Right
Twenty Hot Potatoes Christians Are Afraid to Touch
You Can Make a Difference

Is Jesus a Republican or a Democrat?

Is Jesus a
Republican
or a
Democrat?

and 14 Other Polarizing Issues

Tony Campolo

WORD PUBLISHING

DALLAS LONDON VANCOUVER MELBOURNE

PUBLISHED BY WORD PUBLISHING,
DALLAS, TEXAS

Unless otherwise indicated, Scripture quotations used in this book are
from the King James Version of the Bible.

Other references are from the following sources:
Holy Bible, New Century Version (NCV), copyright © 1987, 1988,
1991 by Word Publishing, Dallas, Texas 75234. Used by permission.
The Holy Bible, New International Version (NIV). Copyright © 1973, 1978,
1984 International Bible Society. Used by permission of Zondervan Bible
Publishers. *The Living Bible* (TLB), copyright © 1971 by Tyndale
House Publishers, Wheaton, Ill. Used by permission.

Book design by Mark McGarry
Set in Baskerville

LIBRARY OF CONGRESS CATALOGING-IN-PUBLICATION DATA
Campolo, Anthony
Is Jesus a Republican or a Democrat?: and 14 other
polarizing issues / Tony Campolo.
p.   cm.   Includes bibliographical references.
ISBN 0-8499-1009-9
ISBN 0-8499-3917-8 (International edition: Was Jesus a Moderate?)
1. Christain ethics—Popular works. 2. Ethical problems.
3. Church and social problems—United States. 4. Christianity and
politics. 5. United States—moral conditions.
6. United States—Church history—20th century. I. Title.
BJ1251.c254   1995   261.8—dc20   95-31479
CIP

5 6 7 8 9 9 0   RRD   7 6 5 4 3 2 1

Printed in the United States of America.